THE
WISDOM
NETWORK

THE
WISDOM
NETWORK

An 8-Step Process for Identifying, Sharing, and Leveraging Individual Expertise

Steve Benton and Melissa Giovagnoli

American Management Association

New York • Atlanta • Brussels • Chicago • Mexico City • San Francisco
Shanghai • Tokyo • Toronto • Washington, D.C.

This publication is designed to provide accurate and authoritative information in regard to the subject matter covered. It is sold with the understanding that the publisher is not engaged in rendering legal, accounting, or other professional service. If legal advice or other expert assistance is required, the services of a competent professional person should be sought.

Various names used by companies to distinguish their software and other products can be claimed as trademarks. AMACOM uses such names throughout this book for editorial purposes only, with no intention of trademark violation. All such software or product names are in initial capital letters or ALL CAPITAL letters. Individual companies should be contacted for complete information regarding trademarks and registration.

Library of Congress Cataloging-in-Publication Data

Benton, Steve.
    The wisdom network : an 8-step process for identifying, sharing, and leveraging individual expertise / Steve Benton and Melissa Giovagnoli.
        p.   cm.
    Includes index.
    ISBN-10: 0-8144-7318-0
    ISBN-13: 978-0-8144-7318-4
    1. Knowledge management.   2. Intellectual capital.   3. Organizational learning.
    4. Businesspeople—Social networks.   5. Social networks.   I. Giovagnoli, Melissa.
    II. Title.

HD30.2.B39   2006
658.4′038—dc22   2006002740

Printing number

10   9   8   7   6   5   4   3   2   1

To my wife and inspiration in life, Penny

Your unwavering support, love, and belief in me—especially through
the many long nights and weekends that were needed to
create this work—as always, completes me.

And to my parents

For teaching me so much, including the importance of
pursuing my dreams; well, here is one!

—Steve

To my sons, Graham and Gavin

May you grow and share your wisdom as two of
the most gifted and giving young leaders
I have had the pleasure of knowing.

—Melissa

First and foremost, Steve would like to thank UBS for providing such a rich culture and environment to work in, and for the support it has shown him through his eighteen-year career with the organization. A special recognition for Nicole Todd, whose insights, hard work, and dedication were instrumental in ensuring that our efforts to instill a sense of collaboration and knowledge sharing across the investment bank were as highly successful as they have been. Without Nicole, none of this would have been possible. And to Suhas Kulkarni, for his many incredibly intelligent and mind-opening discussions on the subject of deriving real business value from organizational wisdom, not only with us, but with key leaders around the world, adding his acumen to the evolving reality of wisdom networks.

Melissa and Steve would both like to thank the following people and companies (listed in no particular order), each of whom provided incredibly valuable contributions to the development of this book and to filling the knowledge gaps across our own wisdom network: Pat Asp, formerly of Service Master; Geoff Begg, American Express; Charles F. Dornbush, Athenium; Ben Dowell, Bristol-Myers Squibb; Myrtis Meyers, YMCA; Larry Mohl, Children's Healthcare of Atlanta; Dave Ormesher, Closer-Look.

Melissa would also like to thank Diamond Cluster and, specifically, Norman Klein at Diamond, for his wonderful ability to nurture and leverage wisdom in an already powerful wisdom environment.

A very specific thank-you goes to Adrienne Hickey of AMACOM Books, for her inspiring faith in us and in seeing the reality of wisdom

ix

networking, and to Bruce Wexler, for his incredible patience and pure writing talent; without them this book would not have been possible.

And a special thank-you to all of our friends and members of our own extended wisdom network, for their shared values as well as their motivating talks, encouragement, and stimulating discussions in the development of *The Wisdom Network*.

THE
WISDOM
NETWORK

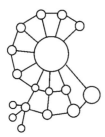

What Are
Wisdom Networks?

Most organizations contain rich and diverse veins of knowledge that they mine ineffectively. Just about every company contains people who possess both explicit and implicit knowledge: the former related to functional skills, the latter involving all types of less well defined competencies, such as how to reduce unnecessary red tape to get things done. Although some of the explicit knowledge has been captured and cataloged, a great deal of the tacit expertise exists only in people's heads. Even more troubling, companies may not even realize that they have overlooked expertise that would help them deal with critical business issues.

The smartest, savviest people frequently spend the vast majority of their time within their functions or departments and rarely have the opportunity to brainstorm with a diverse group of experts, such as colleagues performing other functions or working in other departments. In every organization, people possess astonishing expertise and insights, yet they often are allowed or encouraged to apply their knowledge to only a narrow range of topics. As a result, companies do not take full advantage of all the information, ideas, and creativity that reside inside their enterprises.

Although we were both aware of this situation through our work—

Steve as a knowledge management (KM) executive for financial services giant UBS, Melissa as a networking consultant—things really began to hit home a few years ago. Through a variety of experiences, we became aware of two trends: one negative, the other positive.

The negative trend involved the way in which knowledge management had become nothing more than a sophisticated shuffling of electronic data rather than a synergistic exchange of both information and ideas. In many companies, knowledge management was focused on finding methods to transfer data among departments, functions, and outside partners with great speed, often accompanied by high-tech bells and whistles. Although technologically impressive, this data transfer frequently did little to stimulate creative or effective thinking about core business issues.

The positive trend centered on generating increasingly effective networking approaches. People had become savvy about creating connections with others in order to achieve goals. By using electronic tools as well as in-person conversations, networkers found that they could obtain resources, solve problems, and seize opportunities through the exchange of information and ideas. Informal networks arose within organizations, sometimes virtually in the form of chat rooms or websites and sometimes in the form of unstructured communities of interest or general centers of excellences.

When observing these communities, we were amazed at the high level of their knowledge exchanges. The communities attracted people who were energized about topics and often possessed significant expertise. Although they functioned outside of the traditional organizational structure, they focused on issues that would help them do their jobs better and that would help the company reduce costs or increase revenues in some way. These groups sometimes evolved out of people's frustration with problems in their jobs or in the workplace, but they also emerged around hot button issues; people wanted the chance to share their ideas and information about topics they found fascinating.

Independently, we saw that a nexus existed between knowledge management and these communities, and, as a result, this book was written to help you capitalize on this linkage. We'd like to share our discoveries with you and how they led to the concept of a wisdom network, a concept we will explain shortly. To do that concept justice, however, we would like to share with you how our ideas about organizational wisdom evolved, starting with what Melissa learned from her consulting work followed by Steve's efforts at UBS.

Two Stories of Taking Knowledge Management to a Higher Level

Our respective experiences with the emergence of knowledge networks led us to similar conclusions. Here are two examples of what we began to observe.

Melissa's Discovery

As a consultant who specializes in networking—that is, in helping organizations learn how to use collaboration tools to achieve business results—I became aware of an emerging trend of organizations seeking to capitalize on their growing number of ad hoc groups that employees formed outside of the traditional organizational structure. One company had a thriving online community in which experts in various areas tackled complex technological subjects with great perspicacity. A network formed in another company that gave people in outlying offices a strong voice in how corporate policy was shaped. Companies were beginning to recognize that their experts could emerge and shine not only in their so-called day jobs, but in these extracurricular communities as well.

Perhaps equally important, I saw how companies such as Fidelity, Motorola, American Express, and Diamond Cluster began using both formal and informal networks to break down the silo, or exclusionary, mentality that existed in their organizations. Sometimes these networks formed spontaneously while at other times the companies created teams, but in each instance, I witnessed the contributions of diverse, boundary-crossing groups that operated outside of the company's mainstream. As I worked with these groups, I found the level of knowledge exchange to be at an extraordinarily high level—at a level where knowledge became wisdom. To understand how knowledge becomes wisdom, consider the analogy of fire.

You start out possessing *information* about the ingredients—wood, glass, sun—that are necessary to create fire. Next, you use *intelligence* to figure out how to combine these ingredients to produce fire. After that, you develop the *knowledge* to do something with the fire, such as cook food. Finally, you acquire the *wisdom* to use the knowledge for a higher purpose: forging girders as the support system for tall buildings. Therefore, when I witnessed these groups making the leap from knowledge to wisdom, I became excited about the possibilities.

Working with new-hire teams at a variety of large organizations, I discovered that even the most anxious new hire would loosen up when placed on a diverse team that was free of the rules and requirements that govern project teams. The sharing of ideas and information in remarkably open, creative ways was possible even for people who are naturally reserved and risk-averse as they start their careers.

Something was happening here, and when I met Steve and learned what he had been doing at UBS, I realized that what I had observed was part of a larger trend.

Steve's Discovery

As a senior executive at UBS Investment Bank with global responsibility for the organization's business technology service in knowledge management, I was aware that many people at UBS were very interested in sharing information and ideas and that the company was committed to becoming a learning organization. Early on, part of my job included helping people work more collaboratively with their peers, and one of the issues I focused on was solving problems involving knowledge flows within teams. One big problem was the heavy reliance teams had on e-mail communication to support their core knowledge exchanging activities. People were asking for and sending voluminous bits and pieces of information through e-mail, and using e-mail to collaborate with other team members who were located in places all around the globe. The result was a huge volume of data stored in various e-mail boxes and folders that took a tremendous amount of time to search through and that often contained redundant information.

During this time, people on the teams I was helping were using this method to research and compile relevant information into "pitchbooks" for client presentations—documents that detailed UBS's particular experience and expertise in a given financial services area as well as other supporting subjects. Each time a client pitch opportunity arose, teams had to produce these pitchbooks. The problem was in locating and pulling information from different sources all over the world to ensure that the pitchbooks were up-to-date and correctly focused. This was a laborious process that often resulted in the generation of redundant information. Many times, material compiled previously for an earlier pitchbook could not be located in a timely fashion, forcing the individual to re-create what had previously been created. There had to be an easier and more productive way to create pitchbooks, so I organized a small team and we began telephone, virtual, and in-person conversations with the various team members responsible for the pitchbooks. By identifying several key individuals who excelled in capturing information for use in developing pitchbooks and enabling them to find and share knowledge with their peers, we established a knowledge-sharing culture. We supported it with a virtual environment so that these teams could easily find, capture, and reuse the knowledge that they and others had created. This effort significantly reduced redundancies, the overreliance on e-mail for locating and compiling this knowledge, and the time required to produce the pitchbooks.

After this experience, I began talking with other teams handling other assignments and determined they had similar problems with redundancy and were struggling to locate and share information. Again, my team helped people to understand their knowledge-sharing inefficiencies and how to increase their productivity through greater collaboration, allowing them to solve their own problems quickly and often ingeniously. Clearly, the cross-pollination of people around business problems yielded unique and highly successful solutions.

Around this time, I had also became aware of other knowledge-sharing phenomena at UBS: informal networks of people who came together on their own to solve problems or discuss issues. Early on, I noticed online chat groups that fostered a deep collaborative sense of belonging and ownership of issues. I soon realized that more substantive grassroots groups had emerged around a wide range of subjects, everything from leadership to diversity to technology. The composition of these groups was more diverse than most formal teams in the company. They were clearly more inclusive and open to knowledge sharing across the many boundaries represented by their members, and they often took carefully calculated risks to ensure their ideas were valuable to, and adopted by, the organization.

These groups, I discovered over time, had emerged in response to the hierarchical structure as shown in Figure I-1.

Figure I-1 shows how information flows in an organization from its leaders to individual staff members through mid-level managers and so on. This is a highly efficient way to disseminate information. Figure I-2 illustrates how individuals and teams respond to this information.

Discussion and collaboration based on this information tends to remain confined to teams and departments, progressing upward to leadership only through the established hierarchical communication system. This makes perfect sense from an accountability standpoint.

Now consider Figure I-3 on page 8 and notice the gaps.

Large organizational structures create inherent knowledge gaps be-

Figure I-1. Generic flow of information of the organization's goals and targets from its leader(s) to individual staff through its organizational structure, mimicking its chain of responsibilities.

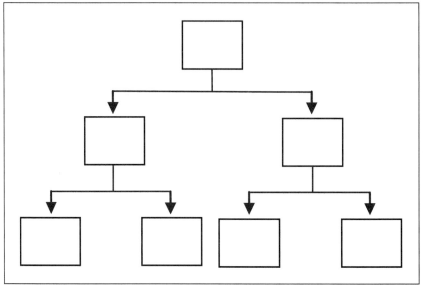

Figure I-2. Discussion and collaboration on subjects often remains within teams or departments and progresses upward only through established organizational hierarchy.

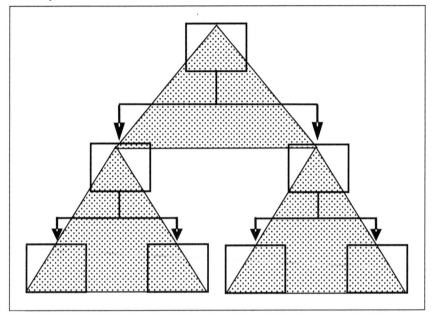

tween departments, teams, and levels. For instance, product line salespeople may miss a subtle but critical advantage of a new product that the engineering people grasp but have never talked about with the salespeople or it may be that the software development in one department or office is far superior to that in other areas of the company. These structures also provide opportunities for ad hoc groups and networks to form and fill these gaps.

Based on this analysis, I decided to do something about these opportunities. As I began researching the grassroots communities and ad hoc networks that had surfaced in other organizations, I realized that these groups could be tremendous resources if their power was harnessed and directed, so I began doing exactly that.

Throughout this book, we will document some of the networks that have emerged at UBS during the past three years and also spotlight similar groups that have emerged in other companies. Drawing on my research, Melissa's experiences as a consultant, and interviews conducted for this

Figure I-3. Large organizations often inadvertently provide great opportunities for cross-departmental knowledge exchanges when ad hoc and spontaneous networks develop.

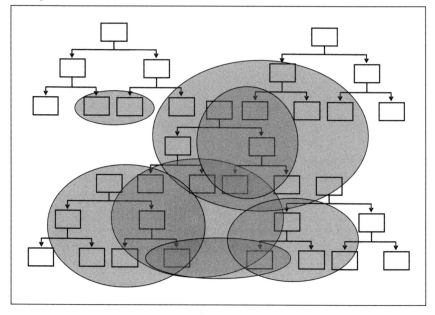

book, we will describe an emerging trend that is taking knowledge management in a new and highly productive direction.

Let's Define Our Terms

What is *wisdom*? In one sense, it is data evolved to its highest form. In another sense, it is what should emerge in response to rapidly evolving technology and information overload but often fails to surface for reasons we'll describe throughout this book. Organizations have so much data streaming through their doors and across their computer screens that they must analyze it, extract knowledge from it, organize that knowledge, use it creatively, and act on it with wisdom. Wisdom, then, is the activity of engaging in using knowledge and the experience gained after doing so.

The term *wisdom networks* is one of our own devising. As far as we know, it is not in common usage. Although we have been using this term in our work, the majority of people at UBS and elsewhere refer to their groups by other names. To avoid confusion, therefore, we need to define our terms.

First, let's consider the continuum of knowledge:

| data | information | ideas | knowledge | wisdom |

Raw *data* are numbers and facts, statistics in their most elemental form. People transform this data into *information* using their analytical and interpretative abilities. In turn, they use their imagination to further transform information into *ideas*. Ideas become useful *knowledge* when people frame and explain them using their intelligence; they offer the ideas in the context of what has been learned, giving the ideas credibility and cogency.

When knowledge becomes *wisdom*, though, it gains real value. Wisdom suggests smart ways of seeing and doing things, learning through experience and applying that learning to gain greater insight and foresight. From an organizational perspective, wisdom can be used to do something faster, cheaper, and better. It is actionable and innovative.

Wisdom networks are concerned with this process of turning data into wisdom. A wisdom network can take many forms, and these forms too exist on a continuum:

| informal interactions | community of interest | knowledge center | community of practice | goal-focused group |

Informal interactions can include everything from watercooler chats to slightly more structured intranet conversations. They may involve a cross section of employees with varying degrees of expertise, and their conversations may range far and wide. It does not mean, however, that these discussions lack wisdom. Typically, however, this wisdom isn't captured by the company and it may not be directed at a major business goal, but even at this end of the continuum, such discussions may produce real wisdom.

If you doubt this fact, think back to a conversation you may have heard among colleagues during lunch in which people started talking about an irritating glitch in a process or system that cost the company time and money. As the conversation heated up, the exchange of ideas about possible solutions to the problem did, too. Removed from the formal work environment, people felt free to offer outside-of-the-box ideas. Although no one may have voiced the ideal solution, it is likely that within the conversation resided some extremely perceptive ideas that might have been the start of the solution. Unfortunately, the wisdom that emerged from this informal exchange probably was not captured.

A *community of interest* is a more formal gathering of employees, which tends to be focused on a single subject; the participants may meet more regularly and attend more consistently. Still, they too may lack a mechanism for capturing the wisdom they produce and the groups may not be sufficiently divergent or focused on key business issues.

A *knowledge center* is a more focused knowledge exchange. Experts gather to share information about a wide range of topics—some critical to the business, some not so critical—but the knowledge center functions more like a resource center than an issue-driven community.

A *community of practice* responds to an organizational need—to an issue—to develop specific skills across departments and functions. For instance, a community of practice may emerge based on the need for project management skills in all functions, and this community's charge is to figure out a way to make this happen.

The *goal-focused group* is diverse in composition and, like a community of practice, clear about its objective. Typically, the group's diverse makeup is accompanied by a high level of expertise, as its members address a critical business issue.

Although this group is more likely to add value because of its composition and focus, any of the groups on the continuum are capable of being a wisdom network, thereby maximizing the value they bring to an organization. In fact, organizations would be well advised to maximize the value of all these groups, beginning at the far left of this spectrum. If organizations can find ways to capture the wisdom that emerges around watercoolers, they may gain insights and ideas that can be useful to a community of interest.

Although any group of two or more people has the potential to be a wisdom network, the ones most likely to add value in meaningful ways are those groups with diverse experts who are focused on business goals and receive strong support from knowledge owners, who are the individuals designated by the organization to be responsible for knowledge in a specific area. When we refer to *wisdom networks*, therefore, we are referring to the most potent of groups.

Wisdom networks, however, are never functional or department-based project teams or other formal groups. Although highly structured task forces and function-based teams are capable of producing terrific ideas, they have cognitive limitations that wisdom networks do not have. A wisdom network often may arise spontaneously, and although not exempt from corporate legal and regulatory policy and requirements, it exists slightly outside of the rules and regulations that govern other teams. Its ability to be innovative and take risks rests with its "outsider," or less restrictive, status. It can cross many boundaries with impunity and gather a group of experts who would rarely come together in ordinary circumstances.

Sometimes we describe wisdom networks by using terms such as *ad hoc* or *grassroots*, because these terms accurately reflect their origins. In some cases, wisdom networks begin as a few experts getting together informally, perhaps over drinks after work or coffee during mid-shift breaks, and gradually segue from this purely grassroots status to a larger, more diverse, and more business goal–focused group. As this group evolves, so too does its value to the organization.

How to Use This Book to Get the Most out of Wisdom Networks

Whereas the power of wisdom networks could be harnessed, these networks must never be controlled. This can be a fine line, but management should not cross over and give a wisdom network deadlines and goals, budgets, and imposed leaders. Companies already have plenty of highly effective project teams. What they lack are these highly innovative and diverse networks.

To help you harness their power, we begin by explaining in the next chapter the nature of knowledge in organizations. Although it seems counterintuitive, this knowledge is not always easily available or even captured. In fact, a significant percentage of it resides in the minds of "hidden" experts. Only when these experts engage in the dialogues that occur within wisdom networks is the value of this knowledge maximized. Chapter 2 will help alert you to the various roadblocks and mistakes that prevent organizations from maximizing this value. From there, we will explore the eight steps companies must follow to help their wisdom networks emerge and become strong, self-sustaining business resources. Each of the following steps corresponds to a chapter:

- Step 1: Create an environment conducive to wisdom sharing (Chapter 3)
- Step 2: Use magnet topics to attract the experts (Chapter 4)
- Step 3: Support ad hoc groups, teams, and communities that emerge around magnet topics (Chapter 5)
- Step 4: Encourage boundary crossing and role breaking in pursuit of topics of interest (Chapter 6)
- Step 5: Identify the experts who share their expertise consistently and effectively (Chapter 7)
- Step 6: Let it be known that people who shine in groups achieve organizational stardom (Chapter 8)
- Step 7: Provide a variety of implementation options to attract the best and the brightest experts (Chapter 9)
- Step 8: Create unconventional measures to evaluate and reward performance and track the network's impact (Chapter 10)

How Companies Have Benefited from Wisdom Networks

The final chapter, and in a sense the final step, suggests different ways that organizations can capitalize on the networks they nurture and how they can help the networks achieve even greater impact as they evolve.

Before describing the range of benefits wisdom networks confer on organizations, we'd like to give you a quick sense of the different ways that they have helped UBS.

1.   As a direct result of greater collaboration across key business units, they have increased revenue, a notable example being the emerging Asian markets where diverse networks of core business experts came together and found new, exciting, and successful ways to meet client needs, which helped to increase UBS market share in the region.

2.   Minority networks have emerged throughout UBS's diversity pro-grams, addressing a range of issues that includes fostering leadership de-velopment, removing career obstacles, and identifying new opportunities for staff to develop their skills.

3.   UBS's support functions have more networks and greater collabo-ration than any other area of the company, in part because seemingly end-less opportunities exist to increase efficiency. These networks have done a great job of focusing on emerging technologies and finding ways to help business functions operate faster, better, and cheaper.

UBS's wisdom networks have contributed to the company's transfor-mation over time in their solutions to the often frustrating problems that arise whenever change is required and the alternative paths they recom-mended to make change happen faster and more effectively. Through their efforts in innovation, the networks have provided an infusion of fresh thinking, as a result of the creative sparks that fly when divergent groups of experts get together.

UBS is but one example; every company benefits in different ways from wisdom networks. Melissa has worked extensively with companies that use communities of practice and other ad hoc networks to improve their sales effectiveness; they find that divergent networks help them estab-lish a wider range of prospective customers, build relationships with these prospects, and give them innovative approaches to increase customer ser-vice and satisfaction.

Other organizations, however, prefer to capitalize on the work of their networks with other goals in mind, depending on their particular business drivers. For some, reducing costs is a key benefit: UBS and other companies we've researched have found that these networks are often astute about how to eliminate redundancy that produces ballooning costs. In other instances, wisdom networks enable the CEO and other top leaders to create a true learning organization, fulfilling the promise of knowledge management. It helps them to move beyond information technology for information technology's sake and to provide forums for extracting real knowledge from experts and applying it toward achievement of business objectives.

Finally, these networks help people to work collaboratively, an increasingly common goal for hierarchical organizations that recognize the value of collaborating across internal and external boundaries. Whether this means overcoming functional silos or forming mutually beneficial partnerships with suppliers, customers, and other external entities, wisdom networks offer a gestalt that makes collaboration easier to achieve than in more formal, structured settings.

As you will discover, wisdom networks are incredibly profitable knowledge exchange mediums. They exercise corporate intelligence by encouraging individuals to go beyond normal expectations of performance in order to capitalize on their innate desire to share their expertise in new and productive ways. By drawing out the wisdom of employees, companies can multiply the value of their enterprises.

We firmly believe that wisdom networks are the wave of the future, and that this wave is building today. The sooner organizations recognize this fact and take the steps necessary to capitalize on it, the faster they will grow their "smarts." Our hope is that this book will give your organization the information, motivation, and tools it needs to become as wise as it can possibly be.

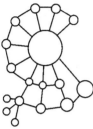

CHAPTER 1

Experts-in-Hiding: The Nature of Knowledge in Companies

Organizations are astute about using visible knowledge to achieve business goals, but the challenge is knowing how to leverage both visible and invisible knowledge effectively across traditional boundaries to meet these goals. Part of the problem is that some of a company's smartest and savviest people share their knowledge reluctantly. They talk about what they know only to people in one small corner of the organization—those with the same function or in their department—and sometimes to only a small segment of that function or department. They also guard their knowledge jealously, fearful that if they tell others their "secrets" their value to the company will be diminished.

Just as significantly, knowledge remains lodged in people's brains or in a company's nooks and crannies because the knowledge exchange system is ineffective. Although technology enables people to send data with astonishing speed, in amazing volume, and organized in a mind-boggling number of ways, it lacks the human capacity to turn data into knowledge and knowledge into wisdom. Within traditional corporate structures, project

15

teams and task forces transform data into wisdom vertically. Wisdom networks do so horizontally and therefore synergistically. When wisdom is produced and shared across functions, departments, and offices, the entire organization benefits.

Narrowly Focused Talk vs. an Ever-Expanding Dialogue

How do these networks maximize the value of knowledge in a company? To answer this question, let's contrast a wisdom network with a typical project team.

The project team consists of people from the same function who have worked together for a significant period of time. Most, if not all, of them are from the same level of the hierarchy. Their backgrounds are similar, they know each other well, and they play key roles in achieving narrowly focused but important goals.

The wisdom network, on the other hand, is composed of people from a variety of functions and hierarchical levels. They have come together voluntarily because of their interest and expertise in a subject. Because they exist outside of the organizational structure, they have more room to roam intellectually, thereby capitalizing on information and ideas from multiple areas of the company. They lack deadlines and specific assignments, but they are addressing a business issue of vital concern to their company.

With these two teams of people in mind, examine the following list of traits and see how each group differs in its use of knowledge:

Project Team	Wisdom Network
Members operate with assigned roles and responsibilities	Members define their own roles and responsibilities
Discussions focus on immediate, incremental goals	Discussions involve short-term and long-term goals
A task mentality governs team meetings	A sense of exploration and pushing the edge of the envelope is the norm
People observe strict topic limitations	Members are constantly crossing boundaries and exploring new concepts

Functional homogeneity gives discussions a sameness in tone and content	Diverse network produces creative tension that results in fresh thoughts and words
Team focuses on being efficient	Network focuses on being innovative
People contribute with a sense of purpose but not always with a sense of passion	Voluntary nature of networks ensures high level of commitment, effort, and creativity

A project team in the financial department may focus on how to save money by getting competitive bids from three or more vendors when purchasing office equipment. The discussion revolves around creating a policy that ensures people are accountable for getting competitive bids. A wisdom network may look at how to reduce overall costs by sharing best practices from five different functions and by benchmarking ten different companies. For example, one expert might share how the Hong Kong division has held computer equipment costs 25 percent below the norm; another expert reveals that the Sydney office has cut its total overhead by 35 percent; a discussion might ensue that looks at how the U.S. group might combine and adapt the Hong Kong/Sydney approach.

Obviously, we're oversimplifying these contrasting stories to make a point: Wisdom networks can produce ideas that are of use to a wide variety of departments and functions. This is not to negate the usefulness of project teams. Without them, companies could not operate efficiently. Yet wisdom networks provide a resource for fresh thinking and innovative recommendations that project teams and the rest of the organization can draw upon.

Freedom and Flow: The Basics of Maximizing Knowledge

Most project teams resemble one another; however, one wisdom network can look and act very differently from another wisdom network. In the book's introduction, we demonstrated that through continuums of knowledge and networks both teams evolved into different forms. However, because we're using wisdom networks as an umbrella term for all the various ad hoc groups that might emerge and contribute significant ideas, we want to make sure that you don't have a fixed idea of a wisdom network in your head. These networks operate with different structures and levels of expertise. Therefore, organizations desiring to encourage these networks must have realistic expectations of what they can deliver in terms of implementing the ideas they generate based on key business goals.

For instance, it is unrealistic to expect that an informal network, which communicates inconsistently through e-mail and possesses only moderate subject matter expertise, could deliver as much as a more structured network with specific goals and a high level of membership diversity. You are inviting disappointment and failure if you expect a recently conceived community of interest, with only a moderate level of expertise, to immediately and consistently contribute ideas that deal effectively with major business issues. Figure 1-1 will help you set realistic expectations of the networks in your company.

Similarly, you need to assess the purpose of each network to determine how much freedom they should receive. Although management should avoid imposing direction and control on a network, it should be recognized that certain networks require more freedom to chart their own course than others, as shown in Figure 1-2.

Three types of networks are represented in Figure 1-2. At the top are diverse experts, whose unique composition and high level of knowledge differ from the norm. They may be pushing the envelope in terms of new product ideas, or they may be a group of savvy professionals from five different functions who are exploring the implications of a groundbreaking new technology. Because of their unique purpose and diverse expertise, they should be given as much freedom as possible to pursue their topic

Figure 1-1. Spectrum of people networking.

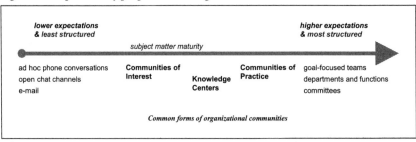

Figure 1-2. Degrees of self-governance for various networks.

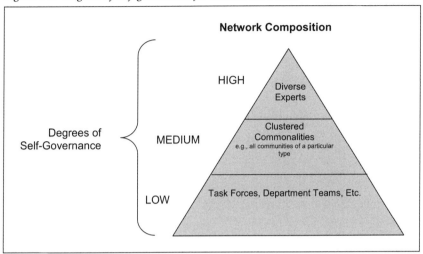

wherever it takes them and in ways of their own choosing. To place any limits on them is to rob them of their mandate to go where no one in the company has gone before.

The "clustered commonalities" in the middle of the pyramid, on the other hand, include groups focused on more mainstream topics. They are less diverse, and their expertise is somewhat less than the previous group's. For instance, one community may be examining ways to increase sales effectiveness. In this case, management must ensure that what is going on in this community dovetails with the objectives of the company's sales leaders. They, in turn, must keep the community apprised of sales-related issues and any changes in strategy that may affect what they are discussing. It may also be necessary to give them a gentle prod in a given direction if their ideas go astray.

The last group on the pyramid represents the myriad task forces and department or functional teams that exist in most companies. They are the most homogeneous group, and although they may include experts, they are all of one type, hired into specific groups composed of complementary skills in order to meet specific project or departmental goals.

With appropriate expectations and governance that corresponds to a particular group's composition, companies are in a good position to manage knowledge and capitalize on wisdom. However, they put themselves in an even better position if they are aware of the third basic element, which is how knowledge flows through people and what to do with this flow. (Figure 1-3 illustrates this flow.)

Wisdom networks are able to perform a terrific job of channeling this flow so that it is maximized and directed at essential business objectives because of the following four reasons:

1. *They are brilliant at generating fresh and useful ideas.* As we've noted, their informal nature, the passion of participants for the topics, and their diversity all contribute to terrific idea-generation.

2. *They capture the wisdom that emerges.* While wisdom networks with strong support, expertise, and purpose are better at this than other groups, they all should have a mechanism to snare great ideas and communicate them to knowledge owners and others in the organization.

3. *They can leverage their wisdom into other areas of the organization.* By sharing with a variety of functions and offices, they become a vital resource for everyone rather than only a select group.

Figure 1-3. Flow of knowledge depends first and foremost on people, not technology.

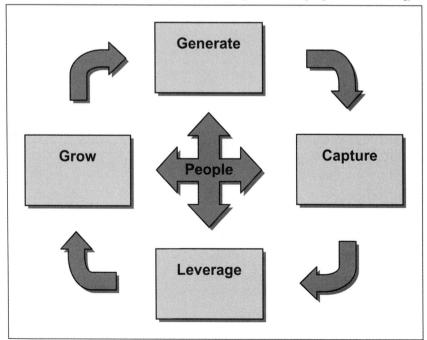

4. *They grow their knowledge.* Instead of resting on their laurels, wisdom networks should evolve; they may expand, divide, or even create new networks. A wisdom network may come up with a great idea, and that idea in turn becomes a launching pad for three more ideas on related topics. These new ideas may require new experts to join the network or may mandate the formation of an offshoot network. In either case, wisdom grows along with the networks.

When organizations have a good understanding of these four attributes, they can derive some general guidelines on how to maximize the value of their collective knowledge. Of course, an understanding of these basic principles is useless in a culture that lacks a collaboration mentality. Experts are much more likely to join informal networks in cultures that have an open-minded attitude toward knowledge sharing.

How to Foster a Collaborative Consciousness

For our purposes in this book, the term *open-minded* means seeing knowledge management as more than electronic data transfer, search, and content management. Indeed, one of the biggest challenges at companies we've studied has been to create a culture that is conducive to a continuous and sustainable exchange of new ideas and intelligence.

A collaborative consciousness depends on the ability to communicate. People need to be highly receptive to other people reaching out to connect with them. They must also be eager and willing to share their knowledge and experiences with their peers, extending their professional networks to others, and expecting the same courtesy in return. We should add that this does not mean people are expected to share everything they know all the time. In some instances, experts would be uncomfortable sharing information that they know their boss would not want them to share or that could be misused or misinterpreted if it reached others in the organization. Consequently, people should feel encouraged to share as much knowledge as they want, when they want, and with whom they want. In a large company, experts cannot possibly know where all the other experts are located, but their collaborative consciousness makes them receptive to hearing from and talking to all sorts of people about key business topics.

Ben Dowell, vice president of talent management at Bristol-Myers Squibb, noted that their organization has developed a collaborative consciousness, especially in its leadership ranks. This is due in no small part to measuring and assessing for this collaboration competency in new hires and when people are up for promotions. Bristol-Myers's move toward a matrix structure, too, encourages continuous collaboration across traditional boundaries. This structure involves an organizational hierarchy that has certain functions, departments, and staff members reporting to multiple managers. Bristol-Myers has also supported the formation of informal employee networks that address issues of concern to women and black, gay, and other minority employees and whose recommendations are taken seriously and often implemented by management. As a result, Bristol-Myers has done far more than declare itself a learning organization or given lip service to the notion of knowledge exchanges. From hiring and promotion practices to structural changes to support employee networks, Bristol-Myers has sent the message that collaboration is a competency that should have top-of-mind awareness.

The ability to capitalize on wisdom network consciousness means continually asking, "What is it we know?" In most organizations, far more knowledge exists than people are generally aware of. Wisdom network consciousness requires making an effort to connect with other people and determine if they or someone they're connected to has the expertise or information required for a particular project. This exploratory impulse energizes the networks, creating a steady stream of inquiries for ideas and opinions that keeps people interested and engaged.

Multiple levels of knowledge management activity make up another important aspect of wisdom network consciousness. The first level is simply checking what intellectual capital content resides within an organization by going to an electronic repository to make this discovery. The second level requires person-to-person interaction, typically involving a conversation with the person or people possessing the desired knowledge or skills. The third level is going beyond discovery by talking and sharing ideas, holding brainstorming meetings, benchmarking other companies, looking at best practices, and generally exploring a solution to a problem based on new knowledge. At the fourth level, the fresh ideas and approaches become actionable, often bubbling up to the decision makers and knowledge owners.

To understand how this consciousness translates into value-adding ideas, let us look at some examples.

How Wisdom Networks Help Companies Become More Than Smart

British Petroleum (BP) possesses an excellent knowledge management process, consistently addressing challenging issues through a timely connection of experts from all corners of the organization. One example of this process involved their oil rigs, which are located in oceans and other remote locations around the world. Frequently, complex engineering problems would arise and no one on a given rig would have the direct experience in how to solve the problem, but the odds were that someone on another rig had dealt effectively with a similar situation. The problem was how to effectively and quickly transfer that one individual's knowledge of a similar situation to engineers located thousands of miles away.

After numerous interactions with people in their network, BP hit upon the solution of a virtual desktop. This desktop makes it easy for one engineer to send out an SOS when a problem occurs, describe the problem in words and graphics, work online with another engineer (or engineers) with the proper skills, and find an approach that will help BP solve the problem—regardless of where each engineer happens to be.

BP also implemented a peer-linked performance process that tied compensation of staff in different departments together. As a result, BP provided its people with strong motivation to share ideas and information, actively encouraging them to help each other and enabling this sharing with technology that made it simple to do it effectively. Together, both the organization and the individual engineers benefited.

Truly effective wisdom networks provide win-win scenarios for everyone involved. They are about achieving organizational goals and providing individual network participants with tangible rewards.

American Express also takes an enlightened approach to knowledge management. The company has found that one of the benefits of its approach is accelerated acculturation for new hires. It gives newly hired executives a three-day networking orientation that allows them to build their own personal networks with their new peers as well as with contacts provided to them from top management. In this way, American Express helps its people to think and work collaboratively. More important, the company sends the message that it wants employees to form and join ad hoc groups that operate outside of the established structure. (In general, it is much more difficult to convince a veteran expert who has never been part of a grassroots network to join than one who has participated in them for years.) American Express is conditioning its people to see knowledge exchanges through informal networks as a normal part of the work experience.

Innovation: A Universal Benefit of Wisdom Networks

Companies that possess strong communities and ad hoc groups tend to view them as resources for innovative thinking and as alternative courses of action. As a result, it is like having all the benefits of a flattened organization without the drawbacks of chaos and inefficiency. For instance, flat structures often result in people going off to "do their own thing"; the lack of clear reporting lines may also make it difficult for employees and teams to know who to turn to when they need help.

In a very real way, these ad hoc groups increase the flow of fresh thinking in the company and also direct that thinking at key business topics. The results of having this resource can be seen in the following case history.

GHI, a midsize food manufacturing company, had been doing moderately well for years, when it hired a knowledge management chief to revamp the company's KM process. She implemented some of the changes advocated by the wisdom network model, including:

- Linking personal knowledge networks
- Fostering communities of practice
- Building electronic repositories of data and knowledge owners

• Encouraging boundary crossing within the network
• Focusing the network's attention on hot topics
• Identifying "hidden" experts within the organization

It took about a year, but when her ideas were implemented, GHI's level of innovation increased. For example, one of GHI's hot business issues was introducing a new product with higher margins and wider distribution. The company had spent a great deal of time and effort to achieve this goal but failed.

This time, however, the seed of a new product idea was planted by a mid-level manager in the business management/financial group. Although extremely bright and creative, he had been reluctant in the past to voice an opinion on new products. When he joined a community practice group and found that not only was the group receptive to his ideas, but it also assured him that the new knowledge management chief would be as well, he felt engaged and empowered to submit ideas he thought might help his company.

Shortly thereafter, he suggested a Thai gourmet frozen entrée, an idea he conceived on a trip he had taken to Bangkok the previous year. He'd sampled the item from a street vendor, and suspected that GHI could buy the product low and sell it high. He did some basic research contacting Thai suppliers, analyzing and preparing a number of possible business scenarios, and discovered that if his company bought in sufficient quantity, there was a great deal of room for profit.

Suspecting that demand for the product would be high in the more experimental age groups, discussion began around potentially lucrative marketing strategies for that segment. At this point, a member of the community from the market research department learned that a high awareness of the product among the twenty-one to thirty-five-year-old demographic existed, thereby supporting the idea.

GHI test-marketed the new product in a select area to the target market segment, where it was very well received. Soon, it was on its way to becoming the company's most profitable product.

How to Encourage Volunteers

As you read about what took place at GHI, you may have mentally applied the scenario to your own company and wondered what it would take to get your own experts to emerge and contribute in this manner. In fact, this scenario raises the following questions:

- How do you get the right people to share the right knowledge on the right topic at the right time?
- Do you connect them to a state-of-the-art computer network that makes it easy for them to communicate electronically?
- Do you remove them from their regular jobs and make them knowledge leaders?
- Because of their skills, do you insist on making them work on projects that are critical to the company regardless of their interests?
- And if the projects are critical to the company but not of interest to them, can they possibly be contributing their best work?

We'll explore the answers to these questions later, but for now, we want to emphasize right from the start that you should not turn a wisdom network into a formal, structured process. You should not force people to join ad hoc groups or tell them what they must do.

Although verbal approbation for people who contribute to and excel as members of networks is crucial, this encouragement should not be directly formalized into bonuses or raises. Encouragement needs to be indirect and part of an overall effort at cultural growth in knowledge-sharing competencies. It means a lot when a leader recognizes an individual's contribution that is outside of his or her normal job responsibilities, and such verbal compliments are all that is necessary to ensure continued participation in communities. People may need direction on how they can contribute to communities of practice and other knowledge-sharing forums that will help them gain valuable wisdom and excel in their day jobs, so providing them with a list of the company's various communities or introducing them to a community leader is great. Insisting that people join, however, is taboo.

Wisdom networks generate their own energy and involvement. When leaders listen to their people, recognize what excites them, hook them up with other people who share similar interests, and provide them with support and encouragement, people find a way to balance their day jobs and their side interests. It's easy to underestimate people's motivation when presented with the opportunity for "high-meaning" work.

When knowledge management operates in a holistic manner, employees recognize that this opportunity can be the chance of a lifetime. For many, it is the first time they are given the opportunity to show to their leaders their expertise in a topic they are passionate about. When they cross boundaries and brainstorm with other people in the company with similar interests, sparks can fly. And when they are able to see the results of their labor—that is, when leadership embraces their ideas and incorporates them into projects and policies—they feel as if they are an integral part of contributing to the success of the organization.

As a result, people in wisdom networks are able to overcome decades of anti–knowledge management bias. In other words, they are able to rise above traditional systems that compensate people based on their job performance and short-term results within their area of specialization. A wisdom network emboldens people to make an intuitive leap, recognizing that things are changing and that plugging into a network can make a huge difference, both in terms of their work lives and the corporation's future.

How Well Does Your Organization Manage Wisdom?

A handful of companies are well on the way to running highly productive wisdom networks, while an equal number probably still operate in the Dark Ages where the networks that exist in their companies are more gossip groups than networks. Many organizations fall somewhere in between, and it is valuable to know where your firm exists on the continuum to help you implement well-functioning wisdom networks, and to give you a sense of how much resistance you're likely to encounter and the areas you need to focus on to take full advantage of them.

For instance, one company might have a tremendous technological capacity for sharing information but lack a culture that endorses boundary crossing. Another company might have a history of innovations but rarely accept or act on ideas produced outside of a small research-and-development (R&D) team.

Whatever your organization's strengths and weaknesses might be, the following questions will help you get your bearings in terms of what work needs to be done. Each manager can encourage the formation of community practice groups and support such groups. Managers can also attempt to link wisdom networks with larger networks, while modeling boundary-crossing behaviors and pushing strong ideas up to knowledge owners. Later in the book, we'll suggest tools and techniques to put elements of a wisdom network into practice, but for now, consider the following paired questions and what needs to be done in your organization:

1A. Is knowledge management in your organization synonymous with content management?

1B. Is your technological capacity to transfer data to the right people at the right time equaled by your capacity to share ideas that solve problems and capitalize on opportunities?

2A. Is your company's knowledge management strength largely confined to homogeneous units such as functions, departments, teams, and so on?

2B. Is your company adept at helping people transcend traditional boundaries to share ideas and work together on issues that cross these lines?

3A. Do you have communities of practice and other knowledge-sharing groups that often focus on relatively minor issues or topics of narrow self-interest?

3B. Do you have communities of practice and other knowledge-sharing groups that often focus on cutting-edge business topics that are vital to your company's strategy?

4A. Is your company's knowledge management process largely exclusionary? Does it exclude the majority of the workforce in favor of the top people in each department or function?

4B. Is your knowledge management process largely inclusionary? Is everyone invited and encouraged to join communities of practice and other groups?

5A. Are there a handful of acknowledged stars in your company who work on all the key business projects and are responsible for most efforts requiring innovation?

5B. Does your company make an effort to bring the unacknowledged experts out of the woodwork and encourage them to become part of the knowledge management network and contribute their ideas?

6A. To facilitate knowledge exchanges, does your company offer bonuses for participation and negative sanctions for lack of participation?

6B. Does your organization make it known that sharing ideas and information across boundaries is a requirement for leadership as well as provide positive verbal and written feedback for people who share knowledge?

7A. Does your culture reward people primarily for results achieved within narrow parameters—for example, achieving functional goals or job-specific tasks?

7B. Does your culture have greater balance in what is valued, where experts who share knowledge around critical business issues are considered just as important as individuals who achieve superior results in their jobs?

8A. Does your organization view innovation as being the responsibility of a relatively small number of people?

8B. Does your company actively manage diversity to increase its innovation capability?

9A. Is there an underlying assumption that people know how to communicate with other individuals throughout the organization and don't require any help in this regard?

9B. Are employees actively encouraged to build and maintain networks, and are there formal programs to teach the science of building strong networks?

These questions are obviously subjective and wide-ranging. They are intended to alert you to areas in which your company is strong and weak, information that will come in handy when considering the obstacles that all nascent wisdom networks face.

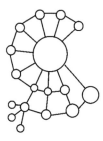

CHAPTER 2

The Obstacle Course:
Clear the Inevitable Hurdles

The ease of creating wisdom networks depends on both the culture of your organization and management's willpower. It may be that because of your culture and leadership approach, you face few obstacles. For instance, your culture embraces the exchange of information and ideas and your company is home to communities of practice, knowledge centers, and employee networks. Management is accustomed to taking innovative ideas seriously no matter their source and employees enjoy helping their peers succeed by sharing best practices and tacit knowledge. Boundary crossing and innovation are essential parts of your culture, and senior leadership views knowledge exchanges as essential to business strategy success. In fact, leadership is visibly and continually supportive of all the informal networks in your company and does everything it can to ensure that they flourish.

Because relatively few companies operate in this idyllic environment, they often encounter obstacles on the way to making wisdom networks a sustainable reality. A results-focused world often requires compromises to get work done faster, cheaper, and more cost effectively. This may mean that informal networks receive little support relative to established project teams, departments, and functions that execute ideas. It may mean that resources are allocated to direct, short-term ways of making or saving money rather than to the less-direct, longer-term efforts of wisdom networks.

Most people work in companies somewhere in the middle between the ideal scenario and one of extreme resistance to wisdom networks. The challenge is finding ways to overcome the resistance you encounter and helping networks thrive despite being "outside" the formal, sustaining structure of the organization.

We have found that many people start out with great enthusiasm and effort as wisdom network champions but become discouraged when they hit the inevitable roadblocks. They become frustrated when only three people show up at a community-of-practice meeting or management doesn't acknowledge their efforts. Just as significantly, some obstacles arise because management has the right idea but the wrong approach, meaning that it endorses knowledge management but goes about it in the wrong way.

Reasons for Roadblocks

In a moment, we'll look at these obstacles and discuss ways to overcome them. First, though, we'd like to give you a sense of why some leaders are wary of the various informal networks that operate within their offices.

Wisdom Networks Often Catalyze Change . . . And Change Can Be Scary

Many people in organizations prefer to preserve the status quo than to try something new. This isn't just the nature of organizations but also human nature. Managers and supervisors, too, are generally risk-averse and usually opt for what they know works and what they're comfortable with.

Wisdom networks frequently recommend courses of action that are new and different. This is true of all innovative ideas, but when an idea emanates from an unproven source such as a wisdom network, it creates even more resistance. People are more likely to see the immediate costs of innovation than future savings or moneymaking possibilities. For some managers, the switching costs are too high. When investment and commitment must be made to create a new product, service, or process, people instinctively resist.

Therefore, be prepared for the naysayers' objections to ideas that come out of wisdom networks. These objections will fade away as networks prove their worth, but initially, you should expect resistance. To counter this resistance, be prepared for objections when a network-produced idea is presented and the possibility of change is raised. Anticipate the reasons for the objections and have counterarguments ready.

Too often, ad hoc groups are so excited about their idea and so convinced of its value that they believe it will be received warmly. This is rarely the case, especially if significant change is called for. Ask yourself why functional heads or other executives might find the change off-putting. Form a counterargument that reassures these people that you have anticipated and have solutions for the problems they have raised and also present them with the benefits to their particular functions as well as to the organization as a whole. Most often, if wisdom networks can anticipate objections, they can overcome the resistance.

Red Flags: Policies and Attitudes That Discourage Wisdom Networks

The good news is that even in virulently anti–knowledge-sharing cultures, some form of knowledge exchange exists. Savvy people communicate with each other about new or better ways of doing things no matter how repressive the culture. On the golf course, around the coffee machine, or over drinks after work, astute employees instinctively and informally share their ideas about how to reduce turnover, commiserate on personal work-life issues, and come up with ingenious new product and service ideas.

The company's goal should be to provide support and encouragement for these informal networks, as unpolished, unfocused, uncoordinated, and ineffectual as they might seem. Your company may not be virulently anti-knowledge, but it probably has a number of neglected grassroots groups. Recognize that even if these ad hoc gatherings seem insignificant on the surface, their conversations are likely rich with creativity and knowledge.

To help your organization start capitalizing on its creativity and knowledge, it is essential to be aware of red flags that keep these ad hoc groups invisible and impotent. Do any of the following red flags apply to your organization?

1. Policies sometimes encourage people to hoard knowledge

Wisdom networks don't work well when people feel that it is not in their best interest to share information and ideas. The real experts may choose not to participate for many reasons. They may believe that sharing their expertise and providing access to their professional contacts will jeopardize their careers. They might worry that their proprietary knowledge is what makes them valuable to organizations, and, therefore, believe that the more of their knowledge they give away, the less they will be paid. In many cases, this belief is reinforced by company compensation practices, which encourage people to keep their knowledge tightly held. Compensation packages may be designed to promote competition rather than coopera-tion, rewarding people only when they increase revenue or reduce costs. As a result, people are not encouraged to share what they know with other functions.

Experts may also be reluctant to expend extra effort by participating in communities, engaging in mentoring activities, or becoming involved in other knowledge-sharing forums. They feel overwhelmed by their everyday workload and unable to spare the time necessary to become actively in-volved in these informal activities.

If collaboration isn't a competency that affects hiring, promotions, and remuneration—or if individuals who are unwilling to collaborate cross functionally often receive promotions and power—then people will naturally be leery of telling others what they know. Free-flowing idea cre-ation, active engagement of the members, and a real desire to work to-gether to make change happen are core ingredients to successful knowledge exchanges.

Sometimes, companies can inadvertently change from organizations where knowledge flows freely across boundaries to ones where knowledge flows sluggishly.

Charles Dornbush, formerly an executive vice president of marketing at Fidelity Investments and now CEO of Athenium, talked about how Fidelity's rapid growth discouraged the same level of collaboration that existed when it was a smaller company. Early on, Fidelity rewarded managers with incentive shares of the company based on its overall share price. Collaboration was encouraged because all managers benefited if the company did well, and so managers were eager to help others out, no matter what area of the company they represented. According to Dornbush, while Fidelity is a great place to work, it discovered what many other rapidly growing companies have experienced, that "as the company grew more divisionalized, compensation shifted to favor performance goals of each division, creating additional barriers to collaboration outside or across [boundaries]."

2. Segregated work units can keep different types of people apart

Companies that routinely chain people to their functions or departments and discourage interactions with so-called outsiders make it difficult to exchange the diversity of knowledge that leads to wisdom. Different backgrounds, cultures, races, sexes, experience levels, or any difference among people provides the atmosphere for innovation to thrive. When too much like-mindedness is prevalent, new thoughts are hard to come by. A follow-the-leader mentality is fostered, robbing individuals of opportunities to explore their own innovative ideas.

3. Senior leaders don't model or support knowledge exchanges

When leadership fails to communicate clearly that it endorses communities, knowledge exchanges, and other networks that have arisen, it is difficult to make them visible and valuable to the business. When leaders are unaware even of the existence of informal communities or when they never acknowledge them in memos or in talks, members of these groups become disheartened.

In addition, because they exist outside of the organizational structure, communities and ad hoc groups frequently lack their own budgets to engage in activities that require funding. As a result, they are limited in what they may engage in or are dependent on having people who control their own budgets share some of it to support the network. Securing financial support for the community as a whole, therefore, can be difficult at times.

In fact, some company executives view these communities as "frivolous" and "tangential" and refuse to back them with even a small allocation of funds. Department heads sometimes look at the cross-functional nature of communities and cannot see the value of spending money budgeted for their own department on activities involving other departments. Because department heads are worried that they don't possess a sufficient budget to meet their own needs, they don't want to "waste" a portion of it for outside purposes.

4. Cultures of exclusion discourage participation in informal groups of any kind

People feel that no matter what they do, they are not really included in helping to ensure the strategic success of the organization. Some traditional pyramid organizations concentrate decision-making power at the top and make little effort to solicit the ideas of people elsewhere in the organization. An autocratic management mind-set discourages people from expending their time and energy by participating in communities. Traditional structures, however, don't have to be autocratic. It is a myth that hierarchies are inherently exclusionary. In fact, leaders can foster cultures of inclusion within even the most tightly structured organization as long as they recognize informal networks, reward participation in them, and celebrate their ideas and successes.

5. Employee development programs don't exist or don't emphasize knowledge-sharing competencies

When influencing, persuading, mentoring, networking, or sharing knowledge aren't critical competencies evaluated in performance reviews, and when staff training and development don't emphasize these competencies, people are discouraged from contributing to others their knowledge that could benefit the company's performance. At Bristol-Myers, on the other hand, leadership evaluation is based on excellence in seven competencies, four of which measure knowledge sharing.

6. *Ideas must be developed through the proper channels*

Wisdom networks thrive when people believe that a breakthrough idea will be recognized and used, especially if it originates from an individual or group that is not directly responsible for ensuring that it does. In other words, people working in a community of interest believe that if they come up with a truly powerful concept, it will be recognized and possibly turned into a project or program.

7. *Management lacks commitment to knowledge management*

Many knowledge management initiatives start with great excitement and enthusiasm and then peter out as people take their eyes off the ball, fall into their job routines, and no longer make the effort necessary to sustain the initiative and lift it into the wisdom stratosphere. When an organization's leadership demonstrates an ongoing commitment to the initiative, however, it is enough to overcome lost interest, blurred focus, and a lack of involvement.

The best way to respond to red flags is by modifying these policies and attitudes. Sometimes, even a small shift can pay dividends for organizations. Realistically, it is not always possible to change a culture of exclusion overnight or to break down functional silos. Every company, though, can take certain steps to turn these red flags into yellow ones. The key is to move away from a rigidly functional, exclusionary culture and toward a more boundary-crossing, open-minded one. Of course, this movement takes time. Therefore, we need to consider what organizations can do immediately and incrementally to change their policies and attitudes.

Twelve Ways to Adjust Attitudes and Reformulate Policies That Impede Wisdom Networks

Some obstacles are tougher to circumvent than others. Cultures of exclusion combined with leadership that does not support knowledge sharing provide formidable opposition to wisdom networks. Although ad hoc groups may not be able to get too far beyond the grassroots level if their leaders don't support and encourage them, they still can develop their personal networks and sometimes give birth to exciting concepts. Often, a strategy change occurs and a management team that is receptive to wisdom sharing recognizes the value of such networks, capitalizing on the ongoing work being done on a grassroots level. Therefore, no matter how many obstacles your company faces or the power of these obstacles, recognize that sooner or later, they can be overcome.

On the opposite end of this obstacle spectrum, companies exist where leadership is working hard to eliminate obstacles. We would like to start out by describing a few simple steps UBS has taken to overcome the inevitable hurdles.

From the very beginning of its business strategy to become an integrated financial services company, UBS communicated the importance of knowledge sharing on all levels and across all boundaries. The chief executive officer (CEO) created this vision, which had a tremendous impact on everyone in the organization, demonstrating that the company's commitment to collaboration started at the top. In addition, the CEO and management board created an innovation and knowledge-steering committee, designed to establish principles to guide knowledge-sharing activities in the organization. These principles not only endorsed collaboration across a wide range of business streams but also encouraged the exploration of new, innovative ideas throughout the company and helped to ensure that department heads and knowledge owners were engaged in making the ideas a reality.

Admittedly, not all leadership groups are ready, willing, or able to make the commitment that UBS's leadership did. Nevertheless, we recommend twelve actions you can take to reduce resistance to wisdom networks. Some are suggestions that can help to reshape the culture in order to create a more receptive climate for wisdom networks. Others are specific changes to policies and procedures that can be implemented relatively quickly. Consider which of the following suggestions might melt early resistance to informal networks and later resistance to wisdom networks in your organization:

1. Judge ideas on their merit rather than on their place of origin

Some companies labor under a "not-invented-here" mentality. They disdain creative approaches and cutting-edge concepts because they were created by a competing company, by someone in another function, or by a group that has no formal responsibility for a particular project. In certain cases, management may unconsciously discredit ideas that arrive from unlikely places, believing that even though the ideas sound great, they couldn't possibly have value because the individual who came up with them lacked the authority or formal expertise to work on an issue. Most companies believe that they judge ideas on their merits, but they often labor under subtle prejudices of which they're not even aware. It takes a conscious effort to evaluate new ideas without favoritism, politics, or biases getting in the way.

2. Accept reasonable failure

Companies that don't have this capacity punish people who come up with highly creative ideas that don't work out in practice. Wisdom networks thrive when people feel free to float all types of ideas and when people perceive they are judged on the quality of their ideas and proposed concepts, in addition to what they deliver. Wisdom networks draw tremendous energy from one successful idea, even if nine others fail before that success. Similarly, Bristol-Myers's Ben Dowell noted that the company's practices reinforce leaders for identifying potential program issues early and that this policy saves the company from wasting millions of dollars in bad investments. While this policy must be applied judiciously, it sends the message that failure is not fatal when identified early, and it encourages people to admit mistakes sooner rather than later.

3. Foster a participatory climate where networking is a way of life

Southwest Airlines, in times of extreme difficulties for the airline industry, has remained one of the few profitable enterprises. The company has programs and policies that help its managers stay involved with individuals and groups throughout the hierarchy. The company regularly cycles managers and pilots through lower-level jobs so everyone remains in touch with grassroots problems and issues and the leadership-training meetings are adept at creating a feeling of togetherness. The airline's employees are great personal networkers.

Without this attitude, people are often reluctant to share information or ideas, are a bit cynical toward management, and find the thought of contributing to communities of practice or other knowledge exchanges anathema.

4. Establish a mentoring culture

Every organization has people who mentor others, but not every one possesses a mentoring responsibility that permeates the culture. In the latter instance, mentoring is a reflex, a willingness of people to assist others by providing skill, insight, or knowledge that they might lack. With a mentoring culture, the more experienced employees naturally embrace the knowledge-sharing role and derive satisfaction from helping others to grow and succeed. They are more likely to join ad hoc networks when they feel that these networks allow them to fulfill this mentoring role.

5. Embrace an alliance mentality toward external groups

Some organizations are natural partners, establishing relationships with key suppliers and vendors that contribute to a shared vision and common values, each encouraging growth in local business communities. UBS routinely establishes strong relationships with vendors and local community groups in areas where they do business by partnering with charitable groups, sponsoring arts festivals and so on, and actively contributing to area business growth and growth in community excellence. Not only is this the right thing to do, it also helps to establish the company as a community leader that genuinely cares about its fellow business peers and customers. This external alliance mentality encourages partnering in informal internal groups, so that partnering becomes a standard way of solving problems and taking advantage of opportunities, whether they exist outside of the company or within it.

6. Recognize that knowledge exchanges generate a superior ROI

When companies devote a large part of their knowledge management attention to whiz-bang technology and get bogged down in discussions about how much a knowledge management solution will cost, they inadvertently push wisdom networks into the background. As important as it is to control these costs, these discussions divert attention from where it should be directed—that is, on educating people about the need to share ideas and on giving direct and indirect support to the formation and expansion of networks.

Certainly, valuable and productive technology is important, but it should follow the emergence of wisdom networks, not precede them. When organizations see the tremendous value wisdom networks confer, they recognize the need to allocate a certain amount of money for the right technology.

The big obstacle to taking a KM system into the realm of wisdom is motivating a critical mass of employees to buy into the concept. When a sufficient number of people are excited about working on pet projects that are also important to the business—and when they see how such contributions will benefit the company and their careers—the system springs to life. When the emphasis is on the technology, however, it lies there like the lifeless machine it is.

7. Make knowledge sharing a competency

Many times, lip service is paid to knowledge sharing but everyone knows it's not really that important. Making it a competency that is measured for and used in performance reviews elevates its status. Suddenly, networking skills become much more desirable than they were previously and people work at developing and practicing these skills. Employees at all levels make a concerted effort to share what they know and to work with others on projects of interest.

8. Filter peer review into performance review

Managers and bosses naturally judge their staff on how well they do their assigned jobs, and since knowledge sharing is outside of their job descriptions, they don't receive extra credit if they excel in this area. If companies really want to identify their hidden experts and encourage them to share their expertise, they need to talk to others in the company able to judge who the underground stars are. People know who is really contributing great ideas in communities of practice or that whenever there is a glitch in a process, everyone turns to certain people to solve it.

9. Test-market a network as you might a new product or service

One of the mistakes companies make with knowledge management is rolling out an initiative without testing it first. Not only are the flaws discovered too late and require costly rework, but this large-scale launch makes it feel like a corporate program that has been foisted on the little people rather than a grassroots one that grew naturally into a large process. Companies frequently ask, "How can we get communities going in our company?" The answer is to launch a small network.

Steelcase, for instance, started a small innovation network with relatively few people that held meetings during lunch. It eventually spread throughout the corporation, engendering increased participation and excitement as ideas bubbled out of the meetings. AT&T started a minority network (open to any minority group) that spawned a number of nonminority networks. Oftentimes, though, the easiest thing companies can do is provide support and acknowledgment for an existing grassroots network. Watching people gather in this community, exchange information and ideas, and come up with innovative concepts energizes everyone. Soon, other people want to create their own groups around a topic that excites them.

10. Be open to the unexpected expert

One extremely common obstacle is that certain individuals get to be stars or the "big idea" people. This is not an explicit policy, but in many companies, the same elite cadre of individuals is counted on to come up with innovative concepts or to launch new projects. To counter this implicit policy, management must be on the lookout for smart and creative employees, wherever they may reside. Time and again, we have found that the people who contribute nuggets of wisdom are sometimes far removed from the action. They may be on an assembly line or in a distant, satellite office; the guy in accounting may come up with a terrific marketing idea, and the woman in marketing may collaborate with a colleague in operations to revise the compensation policy brilliantly. We know of one large organization that had its top people working constantly on a new branding program, and all their efforts came up short. Ultimately, it was the suggestion of a lower-level software developer that triggered the branding idea that finally was adopted and proved to be successful.

11. Use the grapevine for more than gossip

Every enterprise has informal grapevines, and they often contribute in many ways to an organization's wisdom. From watercooler chats to employee e-mail exchanges, the focus is on topics of interest, ranging from commiseration over work issues to excitement about new ideas, and sometimes just a simple exchange of opinion on how things are in life. In many organizations, leadership ignores the grapevine as a powerful means of fueling wisdom networks, primarily due to a fundamental lack of understanding for what motivates and drives employees to participate in them.

Perceptive leaders recognize that they should facilitate informal modes of positive communication. This may mean encouraging people to take breaks from their regular routines to meet with other people, offering them meeting space, or paying for a dinner or breakfast if they choose to meet outside of working hours. It means capitalizing on information technology and letting people residing in locations that are far apart have virtual meetings about topics of interest to them.

Paying attention to what is being discussed on the grapevine is also important. Management can hear what alarms people as well as where they sense that opportunities exist. They can determine if there are good ideas rising out of employee communities and if they should be addressed by the decision makers.

12. Recruit people who know how to share, not only people who know what to do

In years past, companies generally hired for experience and expertise first, and for attitude second (or not at all). If people met the specs for a job, everything else was secondary. Fortunately, we are seeing a shift in this philosophy as organizations recognize that communication, teamwork, and helping others are critical qualities in a knowledge-centric world. In fact, we know of several companies that are willing to hire candidates with fewer job-specific qualifications, but who possess great knowledge-sharing competencies.

Wisdom networks are hampered by individuals who are stubborn, egotistical, and unwilling or unable to work well with others. They may be brilliant, but they keep that brilliance confined in their heads or share it on a limited basis (with their immediate supervisor or their team). Organizations are starting to realize that one brilliant individual may not be as valuable as several highly competent employees who excel in mentoring, communicating, and other forms of knowledge sharing.

Five Don'ts: How to Avoid Common Mistakes and Misconceptions

Sometimes, an organization's leaders are strong supporters of knowledge management but inadvertently make mistakes that thwart their best intentions. In some cases, they fall under the influence of consultants who don't really understand how these informal groups work. In other instances, they simply lack sufficient experience with these invisible networks and make decisions that seem logical but take away from the value of their networks.

To avoid making these mistakes, consider the following "don'ts":

1. Do not confuse content with knowledge

While managing knowledge effectively could and should lead to wisdom, content by itself tends to beget more content. Information overload is a serious issue for many organizations in this era of the Internet and electronic communication. Although technology has a role to play in wisdom networks, it is only one piece of the puzzle, and actually a very small one.

Moving content around quickly may certainly result in incremental improvements in knowledge share and business performance—customers receive data faster and are happier with the supplier, for instance. However, it does not result in the innovation and breakthroughs that wisdom makes possible—perhaps a new product that a customer really likes, for example. Customers may be pleased with speedy delivery of data, and certainly they will be unhappy with slow retrieval, but their satisfaction will quickly fade if larger problems, like a persistent lag in customer service response times, aren't solved.

2. Do not create communities of practice without linking them to key business goals

Art for art's sake is fine, but information for information's sake isn't, at least within an organization. Idle information never turns to knowledge, and knowledge that isn't acted upon never turns to wisdom. When communities form around topics that are not in any way connected with the goals of the firm, and people talk to each other only about things other than work, organizational wisdom cannot flourish. Information available to the members goes to waste, knowledge is never formed, and true wisdom is merely a lost opportunity.

3. Do not encourage a myopic view on managing organizational knowledge

Knowledge owners develop highly efficient ways to run their departments and functions, especially in successful organizations. A wisdom network connects disparate knowledge owners around key topics. In this way, people bring fresh ideas and perspectives to complex issues, and provide innovation while often reducing redundancies through knowledge exchange. A myopic view, on the other hand, sees knowledge exchanges as occurring only within special task forces or in once-a-year brainstorming sessions. In cultures of exclusion, only certain people are allowed to exchange organizational knowledge in certain ways, and this limits its value.

4. Do not overlook the contributions of experts who operate outside of the limelight

Obvious stars are easily spotted, but there are very savvy people who operate under the radar. When companies manage the knowledge of the stars and neglect the knowledge of those who are less visible but who have great expertise, they diminish the potential of their knowledge networks, and therefore their value to the organization. At every level in every function, experts exist who know how to get things done, who know how to navigate through the organization, and who are brilliant at approaching issues from fresh and highly creative angles.

5. Do not assume people will share their knowledge willingly

The silo mentality is often deeply ingrained and a company's proclamation that knowledge sharing is endorsed ultimately may not have much impact. One well-known organization, for instance, frowns on people spending so-called excessive amounts of time fraternizing around the watercooler and coffee machine, seeing such interactions as not adding any value, and therefore view such time as wasted and costly. They would prefer that their employees spend their time "productively" by working at their assigned tasks. It is at the watercooler and coffee machine, however, where employees can meet with people outside of their teams and exchange ideas and information.

Management must demonstrate that it encourages this sort of cross-pollination, It must communicate that building both personal and professional knowledge networks and expanding them horizontally and vertically is a desirable outcome, providing the company's wisest employees with opportunities to share what they know and to spread their wisdom into as many areas of the organization as possible. If this is not done, people will naturally clam up.

Minus that encouragement, sharing knowledge feels to some like self-sabotage—akin to giving away the secrets for which the employee is valued. Why should anyone provide an individual in another department with the name of a key supplier or offer an idea to another team of which he or she is not a member? It takes strong leadership and consistent knowledge-sharing policies to reverse this mind-set. Companies must educate people that knowledge sharing isn't about giving up secrets but about leveraging it to mutual advantage. If knowledge sharing isn't reciprocal, it isn't knowledge sharing; it's just knowledge giving.

How to Overcome Obstacles: What Happened at "Composite Corporation"

Composite Corporation is a typical midsize organization with a new CEO who is a proponent of knowledge management and wants to expand Composite's capacity in this area. As a result, one of his first acts as CEO is to create a knowledge management initiative that not only upgrades the company's KM technology but also encourages the formation of internal groups on topics ranging from product innovation to channels of distribution. In fact, a memo goes out to all employees and a site is built on the company's intranet describing each of the new communities that has been created, the support each one will receive, and the designated meeting times and locations. In addition, managers are urged to encourage their staff to join these communities and take advantage of the company's new and improved technology to share information.

At first, things go well. Because of the CEO's involvement and managerial encouragement, meetings of the new groups are well attended, and everyone raves about the speed and ease of use of the new technology. Initially, some good ideas emerge from these groups, and a few are adopted by decision makers to become actual programs and policies. After a year, though, the CEO is dissatisfied with the results. The knowledge management initiative has yielded no breakthrough concepts.

Perhaps worse, people are falling back into their old routines, and attendance at meetings has fallen off. Significantly, the groups have never evolved into the CEO's ideal of boundary-crossing, box-breaking forums where creative sparks fly. Instead, the groups tend to be relatively homogeneous (by department, employee level, or function), and while there was some diversity at the beginning of the process, the people who were outsiders complained that they felt like they didn't belong and soon dropped out.

The CEO, however, is committed to making knowledge management work in his company, and so he brings in a team of consultants skilled at maximizing the potential of these networks. One of the first things they do (working with a mandate from the CEO) is begin an interview process designed to tune into the grapevine and identify who some of the company's smartest, sharpest people are and what they are passionate about. As it turns out, a number of the people identified are not participating in any of the existing groups, and their areas of interest are outside of the designated topics.

The consultants also discover during their interviews that many employees are not particularly motivated to participate in knowledge exchanges, despite the CEO's best efforts. To explain their lack of motivation, they talk about the demands of their jobs and their belief that the knowledge management initiative, like other trendy initiatives, will soon fade from the corporate consciousness. They don't believe that the company is really serious about making knowledge exchanges an integral element of the culture.

The CEO, upon hearing the consultants' report, initiates a number of changes. The first two actions he takes are to make knowledge sharing a competency and filter peer review into performance review. Both these actions are designed to communicate how seriously he takes knowledge management. To further communicate his intent, the CEO instructs his human resources people that communication and team skills are priorities for new hires, that anyone who has demonstrated an ability to build alliances and work well with diverse groups of people should be considered a prime candidate for an open position. A training program designed to help new hires develop these traits is also launched.

Over the course of the next two years, the knowledge management effort gains momentum. New groups arise from the ashes of old ones, this time focused on topics of real interest to group members. People seem to understand what the CEO is trying to do, and employees make a greater effort to suggest ideas for solving problems, even if they exist outside of their functional areas. There is a sense of excitement attached to many of the communities that have arisen, an atmosphere of intellectual vigor and creativity.

While not all the ideas generated from these groups are practical, some of them go beyond the conversation stage and find champions in high-level executives. In at least three cases, new projects are started based on concepts that originated in the communities, and one of them has a significant impact on productivity.

Technology and Hierarchies: Helpers and Hindrances

We have taken a number of shots at technology, at companies that equate knowledge management with state-of-the-art software and hardware. In our view, when companies believe that technology—in and of itself—can provide wisdom, they are deluding themselves. More specifically, they are missing the *people connection* that is crucial to identifying and applying wisdom.

Certainly, technology can be important to successful knowledge management, and wisdom networks can communicate more effectively when they can communicate virtually as well as in more traditional ways. The ability to access information quickly, to create online chat rooms and bulletin boards that invite diverse participation, and to link internal and external communities all contribute to innovation and effective idea-creation. Although equating technology with knowledge management can be an obstacle, when combined with human networks, it can increase the value of knowledge.

Be aware, however, that when management is supportive of knowledge management initiatives, they are vulnerable to the technology trap. Typically, a charismatic champion emerges engaging leaders with compelling presentations about knowledge management's potential to increase innovation and productivity solely through major investment in new technology. This person secures an investment, expectations are high, and then the return on investment (ROI) falls far short of these expectations. Many times, this particular champion is long gone by the time the poor ROI is revealed.

In terms of hierarchy, many people assume that for companies, especially larger corporations, to be truly and effectively innovative they must flatten the organizational structure or reorganize in some other radical way. Perhaps this is true for companies that don't support informal communities and depend on other resources for innovation. Wisdom networks, however, provide an excellent source for innovative ideas without restructuring or flattening of the hierarchy. In fact, these networks depend on the organizational structure to help engage and benefit from surfacing wisdom. Without strong leadership support, the free exchange of ideas both vertically and horizontally will be hampered in either type of structure.

It may seem counterintuitive, but hierarchies and wisdom networks go hand in hand. Each supplies what the other needs. It is both a top-down and a bottom-up approach, designed to support and leverage the existing structure that is necessary for getting work done effectively. Hierarchies become obstacles only when leaders perceive the formal structure to be inviolate and ad hoc networks to represent a threat to that structure.

One of the best ways to overcome the doubts of leaders about the value of networks is to funnel valuable ideas into functions. When a wisdom network–originated idea bubbles up to a functional head and he or she is able to use it to solve a problem or capitalize on an opportunity, this person's respect and support for wisdom networks increases. Therefore, view functional heads and other leaders as potential allies rather than obstructionists, and work at solidifying their support.

With that last obstacle-related piece of advice in mind, let's examine the first step in the process of creating an environment conducive to the production of knowledge and the sharing of wisdom.

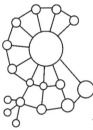

CHAPTER 3

Step 1: Set the Scene—
Establish a Network-Friendly
Environment

We have touched on different ways companies can create more collaborative cultures; certainly, identifying and circumventing the obstacles discussed in Chapter 2 will help to improve knowledge sharing and the creation of wisdom. In this chapter, we will examine how proactive managerial actions can foster an atmosphere of networking, collaborating, and exchanging ideas across boundaries. Contrary to the popular belief of many managers and external consultancies, these actions don't have to be outrageously expensive or, as we've indicated, technology-centered. Instead, they simply need to help people feel they have the right to act on their instinct to communicate with peers and others with similar interests or experiences.

Creating this environment is easier said than done; at least in part because it is difficult for many people to picture this environment if they've never experienced it. To help you picture it, let's use a metaphor. Consider for a moment that an untapped diamond mine exists within each organization, one that is rarely glimpsed and has been only partially mapped and mined, yet one that could yield incredible benefits if fully explored.

Although companies may be great at capitalizing on their intelligence within functions and other well-defined boundaries, the horizontal wealth of knowledge sharing goes undiscovered. All communities, knowledge centers, and other informal networks contain tremendous amounts of wisdom, but the environments in companies are such that only a fraction of this wisdom is mined.

People often guard their ideas and inside information jealously, inclined to release knowledge in dribs and drabs as it benefits them or maybe on a need-to-know basis. And, as we've pointed out earlier, there are many managers who inadvertently encourage this miserly approach to information sharing by rewarding this behavior. They are forgetting that their people's value to the company is directly proportional not just to their knowledge but, most important, how they use it. In many organizations, the environment is such that experts feel that the smart thing to do is hoard information. They assume that their "secret knowledge" is what gives them a competitive edge.

To challenge this belief directly would require incredible effort and cost, and potentially still not yield the knowledge-sharing results that are desired. Threatened by such an approach, a company's experts may only end up feeling alienated and ultimately opt to leave for another company. Therefore, organizations must take a less direct and more environmental approach when they attempt to stimulate more knowledge exchanges.

Instead of telling people they must share what they know, presenting them with opportunities for doing so and showing them how they can gain from doing so is an incredibly powerful means of overcoming this obstacle. When Motorola started its women's network, hundreds of employees joined within weeks of its inception, an especially instructive statistic since Motorola has a classic engineering culture, a culture that on the surface may seem technology-focused rather than community-oriented. By making this network available to employees and encouraging those employees to share their knowledge with each other for mutual benefit, Motorola helped to change the environment a bit.

Environments conducive to wisdom sharing aren't built in a day, but they can be built relatively quickly, depending on a company's strategy and objectives. Let's begin by looking at an environmental imperative for all organizations.

Sustainability: Sharing Knowledge Cannot Be the Flavor of the Month

More than one organization has launched knowledge management initiatives with great fanfare, only to allow them to fade from corporate consciousness after a period of time. Wisdom networks can easily fall into the same trap. In many cases, initiatives fall far short of expectations and promises because they were based on the false assumption that knowledge management is about a technological solution, not an evolution in organizational learning and knowledge sharing. These organizations invested heavily in purchasing new technology, tailoring it to their organizational work flows, and making it available throughout the company. When such investments did not catalyze the type of free-flowing exchange of ideas that many people envisioned, disillusionment with knowledge management set in.

Other organizations grasped the cultural growth aspects of successful KM initiatives and forced people to cross boundaries, join communities, and use all the technological capabilities available to them in order to communicate and share knowledge effectively. However, when the leaders of these organizations realized that these programs demanded huge investments, both financially and in terms of other resources, and discovered that change was slow to come (if it came at all), interest waned.

When employees view knowledge management as the flavor of the month, the environment is poisoned against it. To extend the metaphor, knowledge exchanges become distasteful to employees, who rapidly turn cynical, and view them as a distraction from their work and a tremendous waste of time and energy. They assume that the organization will be excited about some other initiative in a few months and forget all about their entreaties for people to share ideas. All these factors contribute to negative perceptions of knowledge sharing and directly reinforce the age-old—and highly dangerous to the company—adage that "knowledge is power."

Real wisdom emerges over time, through experience and with sustained effort. Although you can usually motivate people to throw information back and forth electronically, you can't produce knowledge, much less true wisdom, in this manner. For wisdom to emerge, information needs to be filtered through numerous conversations and communities; issues must be examined from multiple angles; knowledge must be gained; the best ideas must be culled, pushed upward, and tested; communities must witness a grassroots idea turn into a real product or program to gain energy from this transformation.

All this takes commitment. Sustaining knowledge exchanges for as long as the magnet business topic is mission-critical for the company (months or even years) gives the process the fertile environment it needs to take root and blossom. Sustainability demonstrates to everyone that the organization is serious about the initiative and helps employees to take it seriously and overcome deeply ingrained prejudice against sharing knowledge.

Ideally, organizations will have wisdom network champions who stay the course. Although no company can ensure that the people they appoint to orchestrate a knowledge management initiative or similar effort will remain for the duration, they can act to sustain the initiative nonetheless. By identifying knowledge champions—people who are energized, enthusiastic, and passionate about this topic—management can encourage these individuals to take a leadership role in managing the organization's wisdom; they can recognize and reward them appropriately for taking on this ad hoc leadership role.

Management must communicate to both the champion as well as others in the company that participation in wisdom networks is secondary to meeting daily responsibilities. However, management can also stress that wisdom networks constitute a tremendous resource that can make people far more effective in their day jobs. For instance, some companies trace back the origin of their best ideas via white papers and newsletter articles or more informally through conversations. Through these histories, companies can spotlight ideas that originated in ad hoc networks, communicating that the great new product introduction was launched at a community-of-practice meeting. These histories also identify the community members who came up with the product idea and address how these members have been able to meet their community responsibilities while still meeting their functional responsibilities. As more of these histories become common knowledge, awareness will spread that it is possible and desirable to serve both function and community. The knowledge-sharing environment is also reinforced in a de facto manner when organizations provide wisdom network leaders with requested resources as well as knowledge-sharing opportunities.

To sustain the process and keep the environment "new idea" friendly, companies need to ensure that these champions are actually champions of company goals and objectives, not fly-by-night schemes. They should encourage experts who on their own have joined communities of interest and other informal networks and who demonstrate a capacity to promote knowledge exchanges to become champions.

Ideally, a team of wise men and women will emerge as evangelists of knowledge management and of the various networks and communities that form. These people will make a commitment to see the effort reach key milestones and organizational goals. This critical mass of champions can have a profound influence on the environment and attract more experts to the expanding network of knowledge sharers.

Where There's a Will, There's a Way: The Role of the Leader

Organizational will, or leadership willpower, is a critical factor for the creation, durability, and ultimate success of wisdom networks. If this sounds like an esoteric or intangible factor, think about it from a purely observational standpoint. Walk into any corporate office and you will have an immediate sense of what is important in that company. Some offices are quiet and businesslike, and efficiency seems paramount. Others are noisy and electric, decorated with wild art, and appear to be laid out more like recreation rooms than a traditional office. These companies convey a highly creative and spontaneous ambience.

Similarly, some organizations demonstrate a willingness to share information and to highly value learning and educational programs for their staff. These companies come across as a beehive of activity, with people communicating continually and in every possible way: around the watercooler, in lunchrooms, in virtual chat rooms, and so on. More significantly, although everyone in this culture is aware that knowledge is precious, they also know that anyone who brings ideas and information into the company or disseminates them is esteemed, and, therefore, they do not feel threatened by these exchanges of knowledge. Everyone from the CEO to managers to young employees recognizes that knowledge translates into profits and growth. As a result, people are generous with their knowledge and have many avenues through which to share it. These companies have numerous and well-attended communities and networks, mentoring programs, and training sessions, and a few of them even have formally recognized and supported knowledge exchange forums.

The organizational desire not only to value wisdom but also to manage its sustained growth starts at the top. Leadership respects and rewards individuals who consistently use their experience and expertise to help others, who encourage their people to share their knowledge, and who use their wisdom to increase profits and growth. Although many companies describe themselves as learning organizations, pro-knowledge leaders and champions actually do something about it. They make it as easy as possible for people to cross internal and external boundaries to put their wisdom to use on appropriate issues, to draw upon the resources of the organization, and to increase the value of adding wisdom to the bottom line.

One high-tech organization, a strong believer in networking, recently developed an extremely promising product with more than one hundred patents pending. Typically, a company would rush this type of product to market, attempting to capitalize on being first to market. This organization, however, has grown and prospered through the relationships it has established and the knowledge base it has built. The company decided to apply its business model to the marketing potential of the new product. Instead of rushing the sale of the product directly to its target customer base, the company established partnerships with larger corporations it considers business leaders.

The goal was to use these partnerships to refine and upgrade the product to maximize its value. Through these partnerships, the organization has initiated dialogues about the product's research, technical design and development, marketing strategy, and product distribution. This company is pouring every ounce of wisdom it can find into the product's life cycle, and it is able to do so because its environment is very receptive to knowledge exchanges. The partnering reflex exhibited here emerges only when the organizational will to manage wisdom is strong. In most companies, partnering falls by the wayside in the face of a significant opportunity, such as being first to market. In an environment in which the only path available is to achieve results, most employees won't consider deviating from that path. When people work in an environment where they feel empowered to cross whatever boundaries exist to acquire the wisdom they require, they have more options to achieve their goals.

In a similar use of leadership willpower, Canada-based Clarica Life Insurance Company supports more than eighty communities of practice using its intranet to provide communication, scheduling, and information sharing. Supporting this number of knowledge exchanges certainly contributes to a healthy environment for the development of wisdom, but the diverse types of communities are just as significant.

For instance, the company has launched what it refers to as the Agent Network, a virtual community for the company's three thousand agents in North America, where each agent can gain access to colleagues' ideas and information about everything from a listing of current insurance products to their marketing costs. It is a true organizational knowledge bank. The company also spreads wisdom through a virtual community for branch managers that is designed to stimulate product innovation. Again, this proliferation of communities is made possible only when leaders communicate their commitment to making these ad hoc networks a part of organizational life.

Whether an organization creates virtual communities or uses networking in bold ways, it encourages all forms of knowledge exchange. These examples obviously illustrate wisdom-friendly environments that have been years in the making. Some organizations are more interested in the practical elements of creating the right environment immediately, so let's examine some options.

Catalysts for Generating Wisdom

Manifesting the will that encourages employees to seek and share wisdom can take many forms. Some companies start off with a bang, by using every possible resource to demonstrate how committed they are to knowledge exchanges. Their goal is to create an environment receptive to these exchanges as quickly as possible. Other companies create the proper environment more slowly in order to test and refine the process. Either option, or any in between, is fine.

Organizations must determine the pace that suits their organizations, based on their particular situations. Some companies are embroiled in crises or other distracting events and cannot move forward with great speed. Others have business strategies that demand they ramp up their innovation capabilities, and they see development of wisdom networks as critical to this goal.

No matter what pace a company chooses, it can foster a positive environment for wisdom networks by establishing core competencies that encourage learning, knowledge sharing, and wisdom growth. These competencies range from simple communication skills to advanced mentoring, influencing, and persuading skills.

Three Ways to Create a Positive Environment

Here are three different options for creating an environment that helps wisdom networks flourish:

1. Add one knowledge-sharing competency to employee performance evaluations

In other words, inform members of the leadership group that they will now be evaluated based on their proficiency in one of the following areas:

- Communicating with people outside of their department
- Encouraging their staff to communicate across boundaries
- Using existing knowledge management technology to share ideas and information with people in other functions, departments, or offices

Whatever the competency is, it motivates leaders to change their behaviors in a knowledge-exchange direction and triggers an environmental shift.

2. Add multiple knowledge-sharing competencies to performance evaluations

A set of competencies provides more incentive for leaders to foster a knowledge-sharing environment. A cluster of interrelated competencies helps leaders widen their focus and recognize that wisdom networks are the culmination of numerous factors; that it is not enough to use KM technology or to hold occasional brainstorming sessions; and that wisdom emerges when knowledge is exchanged continually, supported vigorously, and practiced in many different forms.

3. Add more ambitious objectives for more people

In other words, move beyond competencies to specific goals related to paving the way for wisdom networks, and go beyond the top leadership group to all managerial levels. For instance, managers might be asked to support communities of practice, interest, and development. They might be expected to champion the causes of communities and work at moving the best ideas into the hands of knowledge owners. A second goal might involve using knowledge sharing to solve a particular problem, such as cutting through bureaucratic red tape to get things done. Another objective might be to participate in knowledge exchanges around a hot topic, whether internally or externally.

DaimlerChrysler has employed these and other catalysts for sharing wisdom as part of its extensive knowledge management effort. The company is eager to motivate people to participate in its many communities but doesn't want to make doing so feel like an obligation. As a result, the company has chosen to use its annual performance review process to encourage participation. Employees are reviewed in two general areas: management by objectives and behaviors/competencies.

In this latter category, sharing knowledge and experience is a key behavior that is assessed, and the easiest way to receive a positive assessment is through community participation. Employees are not given a maximum bonus or salary increase unless they exhibit knowledge-sharing behaviors. In addition, DaimlerChrysler uses other rewards and recognitions to catalyze the sharing of wisdom. For example, the company's senior vice presidents host an annual luncheon honoring community members who author white papers and other written communications about their community activities. Awards are presented at this luncheon, an internal newsletter documents their accomplishments, and community leaders are clearly identified as significant leaders and contributors.

We're not saying that every company should adopt the methods used by DaimlerChrysler; however, they provide one option among many for catalyzing knowledge sharing.

Remember, too, that these three catalysts are merely possible starting points. What they will do is create a better environment for knowledge sharing. Once that environment improves, many positive changes happen on their own. Grassroots groups form in response to this environment, while people begin meeting on their own around topics of interest to them and the organization. Employees start making better use of KM technology, and true knowledge-sharing experts and champions begin to emerge. Although companies can facilitate these positive changes, the right environment makes it easier for people to do what comes naturally.

We should add that companies need to consider their cultures and situations before initiating culture-changing actions. For instance, organizations that have a history of strict functional divisions and possess territorial department heads probably cannot take a hard-charging approach. To do so would alienate a significant percentage of managers. For these organizations, it is far better to start slowly and allow people to recognize on their own that sending information and ideas across traditional dividing lines has mutual advantages.

The following checklist lists traits of companies that, because of their culture or other situations, should probably evolve their environments slowly rather than quickly. (Certainly, there are exceptions; perhaps a new CEO may have a vision and the will to transform such a company through wisdom networks despite problematic cultures or situations.) The traits listed, however, will help you gain a sense of whether to charge ahead or take it slowly. If you find yourself making numerous check marks, a slower speed may be wise.

Does your company have

- A history of few if any cross-functional teams?
- An emphasis on results, with everything else—values, innovation, and so on—seen as "soft" or "purely secondary" goals?
- A natural inclination for people to socialize within their cliques, allowing relatively little intermingling among people in different functions, hierarchical levels, or teams?
- A cultural bias toward collecting information rather than generating and sharing ideas, with decision making based purely on facts rather than on instinct, insight, and creativity?
- Leadership that demonstrates little enthusiasm or support for knowledge management or related efforts?
- No grassroots communities or other idea-sharing groups?
- A lack of virtual communities and other intranet forums for exchanging information and ideas with diverse members of the organization?
- Performance and promotional reviews and hiring criteria that largely ignore competency development such as skill in communicating, networking, influencing, persuading, leading, and mentoring?

Is your company

- Completing (or just completed) a downsizing/restructuring and/or in a turnaround situation?
- Part of a new entity (as a result of a merger or acquisition)?
- Dealing with a significant amount of negative publicity (due to marketing strategies gone awry or lawsuits, federal investigations, and so forth)?
- Fending off a serious competitive threat?
- Experiencing rapid changes required because of market changes?

The Little Things That Contribute to an Environment of Learning

A corporate environment, like any environment, is the product of numerous attitudes, actions, and activities. Several key factors that help shape this environment include the company's history, leadership style, and reaction to situational issues. We've discussed a number of these factors, but what we have not talked about are the smaller things, everything from office design to office policies that can contribute to a wisdom network–friendly environment. As important as it is to address the bigger issues, sometimes it's equally important to address a precarious financial situation for a small change program, or the company's myopic results-orientation or a particular assembly line. The smaller issues may be more easily affected, and if enough incremental changes are made, it can have a big impact on people's willingness to cross boundaries, join existing communities, and find ways to get their knowledge into the right people's hands.

Corporate environments can and do change. Most of the time, these changes are subtle and evolutionary rather than overt and revolutionary, but a greater receptivity to knowledge sharing is often the desired goal. Recently, for instance, a top food products company initiated a knowledge management strategy. The company's CEO and team had benchmarked a number of other companies' best practices in an attempt to implement them and foster more innovative ideas for their burgeoning frozen foods business. Unfortunately, people were reluctant to participate in the forums set up by the leaders to encourage knowledge sharing or virtual communities that required time away from daily job responsibilities to attend knowledge exchange forums. They complained of how overwhelmed with work they were and that they didn't see how they could devote additional time to these communities and forums.

Part of the problem, it turned out, was that the company's managers typically drove their people so hard to accomplish already very ambitious team and group objectives that any time remaining could be only for personal and/or family time. Everyone was expected to take shortened lunch breaks and to work into the evenings and on weekends if necessary until all targets were met. Naturally, in this environment, wasting time was frowned upon, and what was considered time wasted was anything not directly related to meeting the immediate tasks. Consequently, you could walk through the halls and rarely find a person engaged in idle conversation or fraternizing with anyone who wasn't a member of their function or team, and perhaps fraternizing is too strong a word for the brief exchange of polite words that might occur in the hallways and elsewhere.

One of the ways this company went about changing its environment was to set aside a conference room for what it referred to as "free-for-alls"—discussions on a range of key business issues that everyone in the organization was encouraged to attend. These were not merely token gestures. They were strongly supported by management. Managers encouraged their people to attend these discussions, and the best ideas to come out of them were published on the company's intranet. More significantly, the company took some of the ideas and directed them toward the appropriate knowledge owners, who then had the option of acting on the ideas. For these knowledge owners, it became a free source of incredible inspiration and new ideas and products. Those wise enough to capitalize reaped accolades, had additional success, and visibly helped lead a key effort in successfully meeting organizational goals.

After a year, these free-for-alls began to be ingrained in the culture of the company. Contrary to early expectations, they didn't fade away because of dwindling attendance, but became increasingly popular and a source of creative new approaches to problems and opportunities. They helped loosen up the buttoned-down atmosphere and prompted people to share their ideas more freely.

How to Implement the Little Changes

What are some of the small actions organizations can take to start making their environments more likely to produce wisdom? Here are some suggestions:

1. Adopt a supportive but not intrusive attitude

This means providing verbal and written encouragement to people engaged in various idea-creating communities and networks but not taking over these activities. Sometimes, well-intentioned leaders attempt to join these groups or ask for reports from their meetings. Generally, this strategy backfires; people feel as if they are being watched and judged, which inhibits their creativity and willingness to propose risk-taking concepts. As long as people know that their boundary-crossing brainstorming is endorsed by their bosses, the groups don't require active participation of a top executive. Companies can indicate their support through small gestures—

springing for a meal when communities of practice meet during breakfast, lunch, or dinner or mentioning in internal or external communications that an innovation originated in a grassroots group.

2. Value learning in all its forms

Some companies simply don't make much of an effort to stimulate their employees' thinking. We're suggesting that organizations should do everything possible to make their people hungry for knowledge and eager to teach others. This can be done by distributing provocative articles, white papers, book excerpts, and so on. It can involve inviting guest speakers, professors, and other thought leaders to address topics of interest. It can involve encouraging people to take courses at local universities or to write articles and essays for publication on internal websites or in newsletters.

3. Distribute "wisdom" hall passes

In high school, students are prohibited from leaving assigned classrooms without a hall pass, restricting their ability to learn what they want when they want. Corporations have a similar, unstated prohibition: People are not allowed to drop their job-related assignments and spend two hours online researching a business topic that they're enthusiastic about or go to another floor to meet with someone in another department about an issue of mutual interest.

People need to take advantage of these "learnable" moments; they should feel that they have the freedom to pursue a conversation about a hot business topic when a great idea occurs to them or if they want to obtain more information about it. If they are not permitted this freedom, they will likely fail to follow up on an idea. Therefore, managers need to communicate that these knowledge-based conversations and explorations are allowed and encouraged.

Peer acceptance, recognition, support, and respect regulates this hall pass system. In an environment where wisdom networks flourish, people make sure that their colleagues are using opportunities to exchange ideas and information appropriately. In this environment, people who know when and how to share wisdom are the norm, and those who don't stick out like a sore thumb. Very quickly, everyone knows who is goofing off and failing to explore learnable moments or offer the benefits of their knowledge. It becomes apparent who is using their membership in a community as an excuse not to do the work demanded by their jobs.

4. Hire more people with collaboration and networking skills

As we have noted earlier, companies fail to factor this competency into hiring criteria. As a result, they hire individuals who are eminently qualified for a given position but lack the desire or the capacity to share what they know. We are not suggesting that companies should throw out traditional hiring criteria entirely, but we are suggesting that they add knowledge-sharing capacity as a tiebreaker when making hiring decisions. Seed the company with a handful of people who love to learn and teach, who relish trying new and different things, and who can create ideas and approaches that are unexpected and unorthodox. These actions help catalyze the types of knowledge exchanges that ultimately produce wisdom.

5. Provide physical and virtual meeting places

Some innovative companies have innovatively designed offices. We are not sure which came first, the products of innovation or the office design, but there seems to be a correlation. In these companies, you will find think tank and creative spaces that do not resemble a typical corporate meeting room. They may include inspirational art objects, be filled with the sounds of music, contain everything from beanbag chairs to brightly colored couches, and offer Internet access and books for research purposes. The real goal, though, is to show people that the company believes so much in acquiring and sharing knowledge that it has created special rooms for this activity. These rooms can be online, virtual, and exist on the company's intranet. Knowledge forums where true collaboration occurs can take place anywhere, but these distinct environments give people a sense that they can say things within them that they may feel reluctant to say elsewhere. And it's easy for them to participate and to contribute their ideas and thoughts to ongoing discussions. One of Microsoft's top strategic goals for its desktop applications is to provide an integrated virtual environment that not only supports but promotes online virtual team collaboration. The company's desktop products are all becoming much more integrated with each other, allowing a far greater ability for companies to capture team and community brainstorming activity, and transfer that captured intelligence into reports that convey that knowledge out to the broader organization.

6. Integrate what takes place in communities and networks into the corporate dialogue

In other words, don't ignore what is taking place in these forums or treat them like something separate from the "real" business. When conducting meetings, managers should mention relevant ideas that were discussed in a particular community. Internal newsletters should note a discovery made by a group whose members decided to do some benchmarking or research on their own about a topic that excited them. E-mails should be sent raising questions about ideas that surfaced during a particular community discussion. In this way, these communities gain credibility and are seen as part of—rather than apart from—the mainstream community.

7. Provide people interested in starting informal networks with a "guide"

We've placed the word *guide* in quotation marks because, as we've said, what you don't want to do is provide these potential community leaders with marching orders and cause them to lose their excitement and commitment. What we mean by a guide is a set of parameters that can help individuals in ad hoc networks know what they should do as a participant or leader of a network, especially at the beginning of the process. Although communities should operate outside the formal organizational structures, this doesn't mean they should be completely unstructured or flying by the seat of their pants. The checklist in Figure 3-1, therefore, offers people in a community a way to organize their group and move forward in a way that feels logical and directed.

In the Right Environment, Wisdom in the Unlikeliest of Places

The goal of a good environment isn't to stimulate the best and brightest thinkers in the company to come up with a revolutionary new strategy

Figure 3-1. Use these categories to help you define your network.

Charter Checklist	Description
STRATEGY	
Define Business Objectives	Articulate the specific business goals the community must meet
Define Knowledge Management Objectives	Specify KM goals the community is working to achieve
CULTURE	
Identify Membership Criteria	· Clarify who should be involved and how involved they should be · Identify what levels of expertise are needed · Determine if there are any restrictions on membership · Identify participants, if possible
Assign Roles & Responsibilities / Competencies	· Define specific roles and responsibilities · If competencies have been identified, include these details as well
Provide Recognition	Identify incentives/recognition process for contributions/community involvement
PROCESS	
Community Operations	· Determine administrative details such as meeting protocol, status and deadlines, material review process, community structure · Identify technologies, styles, and channels for internal and external communications · Clarify approach to sharing feedback with support team and others
KM Metrics	Establish metrics to measure outputs of community
CONTENT	
Types	Identify what type(s) of content the community may produce
Subject Matter	Clarify the focus the community will take on its subject matter
Publication Criteria	Establish a set of criteria by which the community's formal documents must be reviewed
TECHNOLOGY	
Types used to communicate/ collaborate	Identify the technologies used to collaborate within your community

that will transform the entire organization. Ideally, the best environments cause wisdom to pop up in all sorts of different ways in all sorts of different places. The impact may not be as dramatic as a revolutionary new business strategy, but it can move the company incrementally in a more profitable direction.

At UBS, the operations department handles payment systems and settlements. By definition, this department is literally run by the numbers. It handles millions of transactions daily, and one of the challenges is making sure the right information about these transactions gets to the right agencies in a timely manner. Although many smart people work in this department, change is not something that comes easily to them, especially when everything is functioning smoothly.

Nonetheless, the wisdom network environment at UBS has had an effect on the operations department. For the first time in years, people have been communicating with peers in other offices and other countries. They have been exchanging ideas about best practices and pioneering new ways of making a highly efficient department more efficient.

This is the great thing about creating the right environment: An atmosphere exists where brainstorming, sharing information, and pushing for innovative change is contagious. The odds are that the first adopters of knowledge sharing are people in more creative departments; however, when they start forming communities and people start talking about what is going on in these communities, other people are intrigued. A buzz develops around the communities, a sense that something important is happening. Good environments make people aware of this buzz and encourage them to participate. In this way, the unlikely knowledge creators and sharers are motivated to get in on the action.

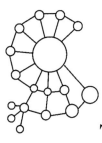

CHAPTER 4

Step 2: Magnets—Create Topics to Attract the Experts

Even in the best environments, the people who possess true organizational wisdom may still keep a low profile. For many reasons, experts and those with the potential to become experts need to be given opportunities that encourage greater participation in knowledge sharing.

We have found that reasons and rationalizations for keeping low knowledge profiles often go away if these individuals discover a topic of personal interest and are energized about contributing their ideas to the discussion. We have seen even the most wary individuals move past their reservations and become tremendously involved in knowledge-sharing forums that are devoted to subjects about which they are passionate and have expertise.

Organizations can use magnet topics to draw the experts and potential experts to them and catalyze the formation of wisdom networks. The process of doing so, however, is a bit trickier than you might imagine. Let us look at why it's tricky and what you can do to make sure the topics are truly magnetic.

Leading Without Dictating: How to Suggest Topics

Issuing a companywide mandate that dictates everyone must begin participating in knowledge-sharing activities such as communities of interest,
centers of excellence, or other forums will not work. Initially, it may seem
as if it is working, since people will naturally comply with the mandate,
attend the forums, and even try to use them to add value to the company.
Most experts, however, quickly become disillusioned with what seems to
them an unnecessary task that takes away from their main job responsibilities, at which point their excitement, energy, motivation, and participation
begin to diminish. In many cases, these mandates are poorly conceived
and rushed into action, so they end up creating chaos rather than valuable
knowledge exchanges. People become confused about how to split time
between their established responsibilities and the newly mandated ones.

At the same time, leaders should not go to the opposite extreme and
absolve themselves of involvement in the process or allow everyone to
work on issues that have no relevance to the company's major business
goals. This is why we keep emphasizing that leadership from the top is
critical to the success of wisdom networks. It is essential that people understand the key goals of the organization and how these forums and the
topics they focus on will help to achieve these goals. Leaders must provide
support as well as sufficient freedom so experts can approach both the
topics and forums from angles of their own choosing. They will find topics
and forums where they feel they can contribute the most and that they are
passionate about.

To a certain extent, how a company "invites" community participation in a magnet topic depends on where it is in terms of wisdom network
development. For example, Bristol-Myers Squibb had a strong knowledge
management program in 2001, but the company was just starting to get
involved in recognizing and supporting its informal networks. The company had recently purchased DuPont Pharmaceutical Company, and it
feared that the acquisition might cause other companies to pick off some
of the best and brightest people from DuPont, resulting in Bristol-Myers
Squibb losing a tremendous amount of valuable information and ideas.
The company was especially worried about the loss of tacit knowledge. As

a result, it issued a call for volunteers to help the company capture this knowledge before it was lost. People at Bristol-Myers Squibb were energized by this call, recognizing that scientific research and processes were of critical value, and 150 people volunteered and worked at capturing and cataloging knowledge.

About a year later, Bristol-Myers Squibb floated an even more important topic: why some of their drugs were approved by regulatory agencies quickly and others received slower approvals. Again, numerous volunteers flocked toward this topic and began collecting information, discussing what they learned, and forming conclusions. This time, though, they wrote articles to communicate their conclusions, which were later turned into recommendations for improving the drug approval process.

Although these volunteer groups weren't wisdom networks per se—they dissolved after they completed their tasks—these magnet topics helped to raise the networking consciousness of thousands of Bristol-Myers Squibb employees, some of whom were experts. The two experiences demonstrated the value of addressing a business topic in an unorthodox manner, and so when Bristol-Myers opened a portal in which space for fledgling communities was reserved, the company received numerous applications from experts in a wide variety of functions.

Next, let's look at how a magnet topic evolved in another organization, and why topic evolution provides a way for networks to attract new and diverse experts.

The Zen of Topic Selection

Consider a company that is just beginning a rapid global expansion, but its progress and success is being hampered by the difficulty many employees experience when stationed for the first time in other countries and need to adjust to vastly different cultures. Although many people are eager to be transferred to gain career-enhancing experiences, they struggle with the differences of living and working in foreign countries and discover that their usual ways of doing business won't necessarily work.

In this example, the overarching business goal is globalization of the business and the magnet topic is cultural adjustment. The CEO or another senior leader announces that cultural adjustment is a key business goal, communicating that whoever contributes to achieving this goal will be recognized. At first, a formal task force may form to address the issue. Typically, this would be a homogeneous group of human resources people with one or two global executives added to the mix. Simultaneously, informal groups—composed primarily of people with an immediate or personal interest in seeing the global expansion problems overcome, such as managers and department heads who have transferred abroad themselves—come together to talk about transition problems.

They are particularly keen to resolve these issues quickly, because not only are they struggling with their own adjustments but they also need to help their staff who may be struggling. Soon they begin to reach out beyond their groups and query others in the organization who might help them succeed. They invite people in from other departments and functions who may be able to shed some light on this topic. They may even contact individuals outside the company to solicit their expert opinions.

A diverse group of experts emerges around this topic, one with no official organizational structure attached to it. A psychologist in HR who has a significant amount of experience helping employees through difficult transitions makes his voice heard. A veteran marketing executive who has worked in France, Japan, China, and Australia also joins the discussion. A financial vice president who went through intensive training with her previous company before working in Singapore for two years also participates. And several people, who come from the new countries, learn about their new teammates and start to help them to understand the cultural differences.

Gradually, the topic evolves and becomes more focused. This group of experts begins investigating leadership-training programs that focus on cultural adaptation for global executives and finds a consulting firm considered far above everyone else in providing this service. They meet with the firm and talk about how their capabilities might mesh with the company's needs. Soon, the group proposes hiring the consulting firm for a test of its processes. The firm is hired, and it does a terrific job of preparing people for global assignments. The informal community of experts reaps the benefits as well, and its members have established a common and binding interest in and for each other, opting to keep communicating and sharing their experiences of cultural adaptation, thus forming a foundation for a self-sustaining wisdom network.

Over time, the cultural adaptation topic naturally returns to specific company globalization goals but evolves further, centering on differences in client needs. As part of this topic, the experts address changes in marketing strategies that are needed; they also attempt to understand the regulatory and legal aspects of doing business in a new country. Eventually, several additional wisdom networks spin off from the original, digging deeper into the details of each of these areas. These network topics, like wisdom itself, are a naturally renewing and changing resource. The way topics change within networks or in second- and third-generation spin-offs isn't necessarily a linear process; a network doesn't always say, "Today we talked about Topic A; now we're going to move on to Topic B." Instead, topics change in response to changing business needs as well as to the particular interests of members.

As you may have suspected, the very involvement of experts evolved the topic itself. Because of the enthusiasm and diversity of the people engaged, ideas cross-pollinated. No doubt, the homogeneous task force may have solved the cultural adaptation problem on its own or may have recommended a change program to help global executives make a smooth transition. At the same time, the group would not have the wherewithal to move beyond the immediate topic and explore larger business opportunities. A more formal, traditional group would have lacked a key element: The real-world experience of diverse experts—people who were actually going through this transition and were committed to finding the best solution by reaching out across boundaries for ideas—who likely produced the optimum approach. The right topic, endorsed and communicated by a company's leaders, can launch ad hoc groups with tremendous idea-creating potential.

Perhaps most significantly, choosing the right topic means creating a continuing source of wisdom. Task forces, change programs, and projects all have an intentionally limited shelf life. Their mandates are narrow and once they have achieved their mission, they disband. Consider the previous example and what the community that emerged around this global expansion topic might do next. Assuming that the company supports this group, the odds are that they would continue to meet and communicate, both in person and online. Each of the experts found it intellectually stimulating and personally and professionally rewarding to participate in the discussion about cultural transition. Each felt deep satisfaction helping his or her organization to meet its goal of global expansion. It was a rare opportunity to work with people with whom they normally wouldn't work closely and to address a topic that wouldn't normally be addressed in this fashion. No doubt, at least some of the network participants will become evangelists for the wisdom network approach in other areas of the company or in other situations. They will mentor others as experienced participants in other groups and will recommend topics that might benefit from a wisdom network approach.

Experts love talking about magnet business topics and expanding the discussion in different directions. In this instance, the network might also recognize that cultural transitions as a result of global business expansion are not the only transitions people in their company struggle with. The participating human resources member might note that people moving from individual contributor to first-time manager roles have had trouble letting go of hands-on responsibilities because they tend to want to do everything themselves and delegate only the simplest of tasks. Another member, someone in operations, suggests that this might be one reason for the rising turnover rate among people who have been with the company for three to five years. A third member might note that he knows of an organization that is providing training for five different transition points, and perhaps they might visit this organization and see what they're doing. Perhaps their discussion attracts another expert, an organizational development specialist, who is aware of a second company that has reduced its turnover by 25 percent by using coaching and mentoring strategies to facilitate smooth transitions.

Over time, this group may add and subtract members, move from one topic to the next, make recommendations and see some of them implemented, and generally increase the wisdom of the organization. They become not just a team or task force but a sustainable resource and a catalyst for new networks. Rather than focusing on just one topic and disbanding, they evolve as do their topics. As new members join and bring different views, they may introduce fresh topics that eventually result in the birth of new networks, taking some people from the old network and inviting in other experts. To draw an analogy to school, these magnet topics offer a chance to participate in spontaneously formed extracurricular activities supported and encouraged by the school, ones that may not be directly related to any particular fields of study, but ones of great and stimulating interest to participants and ones that facilitate the social and educational growth of participants.

How to Unearth Compelling Topics

Although the primary objective of topics is to help meet company goals, a more subtle aspect is to draw experts out of the woodwork and to maximize the value they bring to the organization. When experts become visible, they draw budding experts toward them. As we saw in an earlier example, the right topic brought together a synergistic and highly diverse group, individuals with a vested interest in the topic who were excited about spending time and energy in discussing it. Many of them were crossing organizational boundaries for the opportunity to participate.

Although a topic may not start out with magnetic qualities, it often develops them through community discussions. For example, the topic of diversity may be too general and overly discussed to draw many people to it. It can gain power, however, through ongoing dialogues. Perhaps the company receives negative publicity about its all-Caucasian, all-male senior management. Starting there, the topic can become more focused during ad hoc network discussions, and soon revolve around the issue of how diverse cultures tend to be more productive and profitable than cultures that are not diverse. Perhaps, it may center on different processes that have been used to facilitate leadership diversity. These intellectually challenging, personally relevant topics have the power to attract experts from all corners of the organization.

To increase the magnetic quality of your company's topics, here are some steps you can follow:

1. Allow the community to grow organically

Have faith that your various communities will find and evolve topics on their own. Avoid overmanaging. We cannot overemphasize this point, because organizations are often sorely tempted to intervene and direct the efforts of communities. Because they often lack faith that communities can pursue knowledge exchanges without supervision, management teams may try to take control of communities. They may attempt to dictate exactly what the topic is and what they want the community to do about it, thereby de-magnetizing it. Rather than allowing natural enthusiasm and boundary-crossing ideas to shape the topic, management imposes its will and creates a subject that may be strategically right but wrong for a wisdom network. In other words, the topic did not evolve naturally and therefore people don't feel as if they own it. In some situations, certainly, leaders know exactly how they want to handle a topic and who they want to handle it, and task forces make sense in these instances. These leaders must understand, though, that when they impose topics on task forces or less formal groups, they diminish enthusiasm and creativity. Wisdom networks are inherently inspiring mediums of exchange, and it is difficult to be inspired when someone is telling you exactly what you must do.

2. Keep your hands off, but your ear on the community

Although management teams should not dictate the process, they should monitor it. Monitoring can help them know when they should offer support, in terms of money and technology as well as verbal approbation. In this way, a company can provide the resources necessary to sustain a community and the approval community members need to feel they are doing something important. With this support, members approach topics with an exploratory, adventurous mentality.

Monitoring does not mean eavesdropping or having a spy within the community. Instead, open and honest conversations should be held with community members; telephone calls and e-mails should be exchanged about the group's ideas. Management should be open to these ideas and not judgmental, encouraging community members to be frank about how a topic is reforming based on discussions, research, benchmarking, and so on. Perhaps the best method of monitoring without being intrusive involves creating outputs from the networks and connecting them to the larger organization. When networks publish newsletters, hold knowledge fairs, and schedule expert briefings with leaders on relevant magnet topics, they can keep management abreast of developments, at least in a general sense. Management teams, in turn, must accept that they will receive less specific and regular information than they would if they were supervising a project management team. If they demand weekly reports and insist on written, reviewable goals, they will obtain more information but less knowledge.

3. Sift through ideas

As the topic evolves, actionable ideas may emerge. Although management teams should not kill ideas prematurely or dampen the enthusiasm of communities, they need to choose the ideas that they will take to the next level. Approving a concept that a community gave birth to helps energize the entire community and spurs the members to do more with topics than they otherwise might. It is exciting to realize that the informal online and in-person meetings actually produced something that the company's leadership takes seriously. As a result, the members of this group attack topics with great vigor, buoyed by the understanding that what they are doing has an impact.

At the same time, management must learn how to reject network ideas in a highly interactive manner. Rather than simply saying no as they might in a more traditional setting, leaders must make the effort to educate the group about their decision-making process and rationale for saying yes or no. In this way, a wisdom network becomes more savvy about the how, when, and why of moving an idea up a level. Network members are more likely to take rejection well when the process is interactive, and they are also better prepared to suggest a more appropriate idea the next time.

4. Identify the experts

Certain people usually emerge as leaders *within* communities. They are idea generators and discussion facilitators. Others emerge as leaders *of* the communities. They are the champion advocates of the topic to the rest of the organization and ensure the actionable ideas developed by the network reach into management, and subsequently ensure they are successfully adopted by the organization.

Organizations must pay attention as topics evolve to see who is catalyzing the evolution internally, and who is delivering change from their ideas externally. To help you identify the experts who emerge around magnet topics, ask the following questions:

- Who seems to be a consistent member of topic discussions? Who makes it his or her business to be at some of the meetings and participate in some of the online chats?
- Who is taking on a leadership role in terms of shaping the topics, inviting additional members into the group, and solving problems that arise?
- Who seems to have the most knowledge or expertise? Who is the individual everyone else turns to when a problem arises or when they become stuck?
- Who seems to be taking the original topic and running with it? Who is exploring the topic in new or provocative ways? Who is taking the topic to a higher level?
- Who is the spokesperson talking about the topic to those outside the community consistently and bringing the actionable ideas to management, ensuring they get executed?

Remember, magnet topics are a means to an end. They should be drawing out the smartest, most knowledgeable people in the organization. Certain people should be identified with certain hot topics. Because they are the idea generators and nurturers, their leadership and enthusiasm give the topics life. Are you seeing people emerge as knowledge stars who aren't necessarily known for having high potential? Are you finding that individuals are emerging from different levels and functions who are clearly the smartest people in the room? Are there new topic champions emerging every month?

In Chapter 7 we will go into greater detail about ways in which to identify experts and how this identification process increases the value of networks to organizations.

Allowing Topics to Take on Lives of Their Own

These four steps facilitate the formation of wisdom networks. As topics evolve, so do the participants. People who aren't serious about contributing or who have little to contribute, drop out. Those who are passionate about the topics and have some level of expertise and interest in them become more involved. As people and ideas are reshuffled, change takes place. Sometimes, of course, the discussion leads nowhere and communities dissolve and reform to address new issues. Sometimes, though, magic happens. A group starts out with only a general topic and no clear purpose, but, at some point, everything coalesces and an idea of great value emerges. This is what happened at UBS.

A group of in-house technology experts became interested in an emerging computing technology in the financial services world, known as Grid Computing Technology (GCT). *Theoretically,* GCT would ameliorate the problem of some business lines and functions, each of which typically requires its own servers and software. By sharing servers and software, the *potential* cost savings and increase in efficiency could be tremendous.

At UBS, we italicized *theoretically* and *potentially* to communicate that at the start of this process, no one was sure where the discussion of grid technology would lead. Although reducing costs and increasing efficiency were key business goals, GCT was an intriguing but not yet a hot topic. Still, it was a sufficiently new and provocative topic that drew in-house tech experts to it. The discussion started informally. Although UBS supported the community of interest that formed around GCT, it did not set deadlines or create an agenda of any type. The chief information officer (CIO) and other senior information technology (IT) leaders simply encouraged the community's brainstorming on ways that GCT might help UBS and asked them to come up with any recommendations that seemed appropriate.

They began by inviting various vendors with GCT capabilities to present to revolving groups of tech experts, numbering from six to thirty per group. The initial thought was that the individual community members would use what they learned on their own project teams for their own business customers. It turned out, however, that it would be difficult to find a GCT solution tailored business by business that would yield the hoped-for savings. Each vendor claimed that its GCT solution was best, and each required completely new hardware—a mammoth undertaking, especially because UBS, like most of its competitors, was committed to and happy with a select number of hardware and software vendors. As a result, the discussion topic shifted a bit.

Gradually, the community agreed to pursue a grid technology solution that worked with the existing vendor products. Therefore, the discussion shifted to whether it was possible to adapt GCT to that equipment. From the vendors, the community members had learned that competitors were also exploring GCT and scratching their heads as to what to do next. The community decided to reach out to find peers and competitors in the industry. They found some of their top competitors were pursuing the same course of action, so they decided that by banding together they had the clout to insist to GCT vendors that they adopt a standard compatible with the vendors common in the industry. Finally, a select few GCT vendors stepped forward and provided a commitment to meet the standard demanded by the industry network. As a result, GCT has been implemented at UBS as well as at some of its competitive companies and has significantly helped to reduce costs and increase efficiency.

That's not the end of the story. Buoyed by the success of the GCT project, several members of the community began using the same networking process to explore data technology, which was, in fact, their area of expertise. They wanted to start a discussion around database architecture, and asked senior leaders at UBS if they would support a community around this topic. UBS agreed, and this database community expanded rapidly to more than seventy members from around the world. They are sharing best practices and helping each other when they face problems in database design. They are also holding knowledge fairs and visiting vendors in an effort to expand the scope of their knowledge. There is no doubt that their discussion topics will evolve as more knowledge becomes available to them. Subsequent communities emerged in IT security, program excellence, and many other areas.

These communities and their topics expand at an exponential rate. Discussions can rapidly spin out ideas that turn into value-adding products and services. New communities become sustainable wisdom networks, connecting experts horizontally across the vertical organizational structure.

Compare this with the traditional way a company might have approached the GCT issue. First, they would have created a team—a team not nearly as diverse as the community that formed—to evaluate three vendors and see which one was best. When they heard their presentations, they would have tabled the project, deciding to wait until the technology matured and a new standard emerged. This is a common reaction of corporations: If there are too many barriers and/or the issues are too complex, they table the discussion.

A wisdom network, however, is energized by complexity and challenged by barriers. The diverse perspectives of the participants, the lack of a timetable, and the absence of formal performance evaluations all encourage new, innovative approaches to topics.

How to Move Topics Up, Not Shove Them Down

Despite giving lip service to the notion of soliciting information and ideas from people integrally involved in company processes—customer service reps, assembly line workers, frontline managers, and so on—the reality is that most information and ideas originate at upper levels of management and reach everyone else as policies and programs. Companies do not have good systems for securing input from frontline employees and moving it up to management in a logical, compelling manner. Similarly, people who are working with customers or manufacturing products often lack the time or inclination to talk about the topics that are on their minds or share their intelligence about what's working and what's not. The question is how do you encourage experts in these positions, the people in the trenches who really understand the way things work, to contribute their knowledge?

One answer is to make it easy for them to talk about subjects that are important to them. One huge corporation had a correspondingly huge operations department. Every day, thousands of operations employees helped orchestrate sophisticated, multilevel transactions regarding the sale and purchase of their services. With millions of transactions moving daily through these money-crunching systems, the job of keeping the systems running 24/7 was enormously challenging.

As a result, just about everyone who worked in operations focused on the tasks at hand. While they could see redundancies between systems and ways to decrease operational risk, no one volunteered any solutions. No acceptable forums for doing so existed other than making a suggestion to a supervisor, who also was more focused on keeping the machines functioning smoothly.

Eventually, a community of interest formed around the operations issues. Management had the larger goal of reducing redundancy of effort in operations and creating cutting-edge systems. Knowledge owners throughout the operations process embraced this topic—fifteen of whom began talking about how they might achieve these goals. This discussion eventually filtered down into a plan, endorsed by management, to have each knowledge owner talk to his or her team about ways in which the systems might be improved. With support from management, the owners set up a website where anyone from operations could furnish suggestions.

After reviewing the ideas—both verbal ideas and those that appeared on the website—the knowledge owners brought the best ideas to the operations committee, which vetted them to determine which were feasible to fund. Anyone whose idea was funded became a hero; he or she was acknowledged and praised from the top leaders on down. For the first time, people in the trenches felt empowered. They realized that management wasn't just paying lip service to the notion of wanting everyone's ideas. Clearly, the company leaders took what they had to say seriously. The most knowledgeable operations people joined the discussions about creating more efficient and effective systems as ongoing participants; they were excited about the chance to put their skills and knowledge to use on a system-wide basis. Because of their participation, significant progress was made toward revamping operations.

The lesson here is that magnet topics can draw a wide range of company employees. When it comes to wisdom networks, titles do not matter. Organizations need ideas and information from people with true ability, and it does not matter if they are top executives or those who have been in the same lower-level position for thirty years. The right topics presented the right way will draw out the experts.

From Small Talk to Big Subjects: Harnessing the Flow of Conversations

In any large company at any given time, thousands of conversations are taking place via telephone and online, in one-on-one interactions and in group meetings. Although some of these discussions take place at high organizational levels and address issues that directly affect key business goals, many of them are smaller in scope and narrower in focus. Although some of these latter conversations have nothing to do with business, a significant percentage are work related. People may be talking during their break about a new vacation policy. They may exchange e-mails about why another vice president is leaving the company. On the surface, these communications may seem trivial or like gossip. In reality, though, they may be small topics that shed light on larger ones such as employee satisfaction and turnover.

In some organizations, these smaller dialogues are overtly or subtly discouraged: Supervisors don't like to see people wasting time on matters outside of their assigned tasks. No online support is provided for people who want to have conversations with others who share their interests, problems, or concerns. Employees who do something beyond talk, who organize meetings to address problems that management feels is none of their concern, are marginalized.

If you trace back the origin of a great wisdom network, though, you'll find that its source often was a conversation about a relatively minor subject. Consider the following: Joan and Jack are young managers who are discussing performance reviews over lunch. Although they both think highly of their company, they find some disconnect between what management says it believes is important and how performance is measured and rewarded. Jack notes that his manager is always emphasizing the importance of building strong relationships and mentoring direct reports, yet the people who receive promotions are often those who display none of these softer skills. Joan complains that she seldom does as well in reviews as fellow manager Dina because Dina's results usually are a bit better than Joan's. On the other hand, Joan knows her people skills are much better than Dina's. In addition, her 360-degree feedback—a form of review where direct reports, peers, and superiors all contribute to an employee's evaluation—has told her that she is a good listener and that her direct reports find her empathetic and able to correct their mistakes without disrespecting them. Dina, she says, terrorizes her people into working hard and believes half her group may be gone before the year is up.

Joan and Jack decide to approach their boss and see if they might set up a community of interest around these issues. Their boss clears the request with the executive committee and gives Jack and Joan the okay. The community quickly attracts a wide range of participants, from HR professionals who have been aware of this issue for years to individuals from just about every function. Soon, a consultant and a professor who are both experts in this subject are invited to participate in discussions.

As the community grows, the topic shifts. The consensus is that management is reluctant to change the performance review process because it doesn't want too many managers in place who are soft and unable to deliver consistent results. The consultant shares a study revealing companies that measure for both results and emotional intelligence factors in reviews tend to be more profitable than those that measure primarily for results.

The community makes a request for funds to investigate the results of the study. They want to visit the companies included in the study and interview relevant executives to determine if the study was accurate and to determine if the performance review measures used are transferable.

After receiving financial support and conducting interviews, community members are excited about what they have discovered. They immediately begin designing a pilot program to test a revamped performance review process in one department. The CEO, who is a results-oriented leader, hears about this pilot program and talks to the community members who have been directly involved in its creation. His primary goal is improving performance company-wide, and based on what he learns from the community members, he sees a more holistic review process as possibly helping to achieve this goal and so gives his approval.

Wisely, the CEO intervened but didn't interfere in the community's process. He never committed the sin of pushing the group in a direction he favored or demanding to know when they would have their work done. Instead, he displayed interest and offered support, the type of leadership behavior that inspires and drives wisdom networks. Although leaders should always refrain from telling networks what to do and how to do it, they should feel free to ask questions and offer encouragement. This is true when a CEO becomes aware of a solid wisdom network or happens to overhear a lunchroom conversation.

Certainly not all lunchtime conversations between the Jacks and Joans escalate into big business topics and concomitant programs. Still, it is important to encourage and support these small topic conversations. It may be that the people who originated the conversations are not the experts. Jack was far less prominent in the community than Joan was. They provided the spark, however, and as the topic gathered momentum, it attracted the experts it needed to sustain that momentum.

It is sometimes difficult to see how seemingly idle conversations about low-level issues could translate into programs that reduce costs or increase productivity. It requires that certain leap of faith, which is the first step toward increasing topic magnetism. Trust that your people will demonstrate the will and creativity to move a small topic into a larger one, and at least some of the time, your trust will be rewarded.

Broadening Your Perspective: Organizational Issues Through a Wide Lens

Companies fall into patterns in the way that they address issues. They tend to rely on the same people or teams to address the same topics in the same ways. If a company wants to look at the viability of an emerging market, it typically creates a team of marketing, financial, and other executives to investigate the possibilities. This is fine.

What is better than fine, though, is when a parallel discussion is taking place. Maybe a highly unlikely gathering of individuals starts talking about the possibility of selling a product line in China because some of them have either visited or lived there and are convinced it would be a highly receptive market. They will go at the topic from a different perspective than a task force would and bring their personal experiences and their diverse expertise to bear on the issue. They may come to the wrong conclusion because they lack the data and the analytical rigor that the task force possesses. On the other hand, their fresh perspective may provide insights that the task force can use, insights the task force probably would not have gained without this alternative viewpoint.

At the very least, organizations that encourage parallel conversations on a range of business topics foster an atmosphere of idea-generation and learning. Given the nature of organizational politics and conservative cultures, some people are naturally going to be more honest in their own communities than in more formal team meetings. In a team forum, they may hold their thoughts in check, fearing censure if they voice a controversial opinion. Freed from being on the record, they frequently can confront issues squarely. Rather than worrying about stepping on someone's toes, they will say that the company has a glass ceiling for women or that the CEO's treasured Six Sigma isn't as effective as it might be.

Getting the chance to talk openly on a range of topics is healthy not just for the organization but for individuals. People need forums to discuss everything from their careers to diversity problems to their need for upgraded computer systems. We have talked a great deal about communities but have said relatively little about a sense of community. When topics are being discussed continually in an organization, people have a much greater feeling of belonging. When they have the chance to put their two cents in, and on the occasions when their two cents evolves into a successful $2 million program, they feel like insiders. This helps morale by increasing the retention of expertise and decreasing turnover.

It also is worth remembering that experts are sometimes hard to spot or to induce to come out of hiding. The more topics of conversation going on in your organization, the more likely these experts will emerge. Given a range of topics and opportunities to participate, these individuals will find something that strikes their fancy and causes them to contribute their great knowledge to the discussion.

What Are People Talking About in Your Company?

This question is sometimes difficult to answer. Although a company's leaders may have a general sense of the buzz among their staff, they don't always know the specifics or how widespread the conversations are. If you aspire to have flourishing wisdom networks in your company, you should be aware of what conversations are in the air. In this way, you can determine whether you need to make environmental changes or increase your support of communities to get people talking across hallways, functions, and other boundaries.

Here are some ways you can tune in to the topics being discussed:

1. Monitor the chatter in cyberspace

If your company has a website with forums for employee discussions, drop into chat rooms and look at the topics being addressed. Take a look at online communities and their areas of interest. Send e-mail to people in different functions at different levels and ask what they and their peers are discussing. Does it seem like a lot of discussion exists about many key topics? Or, is everyone focused on one or two topics of narrow self-interest? Remember, organizations aren't viewed as controlling unless they attempt to use what they hear to change the direction of an online discussion or project. Employees expect management to be aware of what is going on. More than that, they recognize that maintaining this awareness is management's responsibility.

2. Talk directly to members of communities

Assuming your company has these communities or is planning to start them, this is easy to do. Don't be intrusive or judgmental. Asking neutral questions—ones that are free of negative or skeptical attitudes—is always a good way of connecting. Offering verbal support is always appreciated. If communities seem to be going off course, you can engage them in a discussion where you express your concerns and explore why they may be going down a blind alley. Keep in mind, though, that your role is not to set a direction for the community or impose parameters on it. The goal of your conversation is to get a read on the issues communities are grappling with and to register continued interest in the community's members. Do members feel they are making progress? Do they find the discussions stimulating and the ideas cutting edge? Or, are members of these communities bored by the discussions and find they are going over the same ground they've covered as part of their day jobs?

3. Trace back the source of big ideas

In the past year or two, your company has probably had a number of successful ventures, programs, and policies. Perhaps you have launched a new hiring strategy that has brought in a great deal of young talent. Maybe you have revamped the software in a division and it has dramatically improved efficiency and ease of use. Take two or three of these successes and trace back where the ideas originated. This requires a bit of spadework, but it usually isn't difficult to discover who catalyzed a successful venture. Did the success start out in a community of interest or other discussion group within the organization? Did it begin as a small thing, a simple suggestion from one or two people down in the rank and file or an interesting bit of research, and was it nurtured through conversation into something much more significant and with great impact?

Don't be discouraged if your research reveals a low level of conversation. Keep in mind that your experts are probably deeply embedded in their functions and at behind-the-scenes positions. It may be that to bring them out, you just need to offer additional support. As you'll discover in Chapter 5, you have numerous options for offering this support.

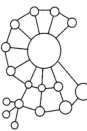

Step 3: Support Systems—
Nurture Communities That
Emerge Around Magnet Topics

Even if you completely ignore them, the ad hoc groups and grassroots networks in your company will continue to exist. As we saw, magnet topics naturally pull people into communities of interest. Without additional organizational support and the backing of management, however, these communities will fly under the radar and the company will not derive the maximum value from them.

Organizational support, therefore, enhances the value of the various informal and possibly heretofore invisible networks in your company. Using verbal, marketing, monetary, technological, and other forms of support, companies can help bring to the surface wisdom that otherwise would never see the light of day.

Support may seem like a no-brainer; however, most companies don't support their informal communities adequately enough to grow them into powerful wisdom networks. Because they are not part of the formal structure, they lack budgets and sponsors. It takes a certain amount of faith in their viability before leaders come forth and formally sponsor these invisible networks, find funds to further their purpose, encourage the development of their champions, and ensure the successful career progression of their community experts.

We'll talk about how to overcome the lack of support obstacle, but first let's focus on eight significant forms of support that, when applied, will ensure that wisdom networks flourish.

Eight Types of Support: What They Are and How to Provide Them

The following sources of support are critical for maximizing a wisdom network's value:

- Leadership
- Financial support
- Facilitation
- Sponsors
- Champions
- Technology
- Performance reviews
- External support

Let's look at each of these areas in detail and what they involve:

1. Leadership

Top leaders of the company must verbally and visibly endorse the strategy of wisdom networks by taking ownership of the strategy itself. In this supporting role, leaders advocate for both the wisdom network concept and realities involved in putting it into practice. They must educate others about what wisdom networks entail, while identifying and recognizing emerging wisdom network experts. Ideally, at least one of these leaders will become a wisdom network champion, an individual who makes these networks his or her cause. Wisdom networks are much more likely to succeed when a champion is in place and backed by senior leadership.

A company's leaders must communicate *clearly* and *consistently*, yet *selectively*, that they endorse ad hoc communities that exist within the organization and their hope that they will emerge as self-sustaining networks. The words *clearly* and *consistently* are key adverbs. It is not enough to offer lukewarm support in a single e-mail to a few people encouraging them to "keep up the good work." It is certainly not enough to issue an ambiguous message that communities of interest are "nice to have, but they shouldn't get in the way of real work." Nor is it enough to make one big show of support and thereafter ignore informal networks.

The word *selectively* is another key adverb. Being supportive in general of ad hoc networks and communities is a powerful base to build upon. Picking and choosing a few that have already been drawn toward some of the top business topics and issues, and spotlighting them with highly visible accolades to bring them to the forefront, helps to leverage several group-psychology triggers. Doing this helps to accomplish the following:

- *Highlights and reinforces the topics that are most important to the company.* By making sure that everyone understands the importance of these issues, management motivates others to engage in activities that help to achieve the company objectives associated with them.

- *Creates the appearance, if not the reality, of "planned accomplishment" in the evolution of these wisdom networks.* This reinforces the community leaders' belief that they are in the forefront, engaging in strategic moves that will benefit the organization and everyone working for it, which ultimately increases everyone's faith in, loyalty to, and inspiration by the company's leaders.

- *Generates increased initiative on the part of key participants in the supported network.* These are the true experts—the people you want to excel. You want them excited about both the subject to which they were already attracted and the benefit it will be to their careers if their network makes a significant contribution.

Leaders must be vocal and visible in their support, and that means using the full range of communication media, interpersonal interactions, memos, online forums, white papers, meetings, and strategic planning to demonstrate their commitment to growing various ad hoc groups into wisdom networks. It may also mean bringing up the support topic in monthly planning or review meetings, or other high-visibility forums, and communicating to key managers that these networks have leadership's backing.

American Express, for example, brought in Melissa to work with the company's senior management team to facilitate exchanges of information and ideas through networking. This not only sent a message to managers throughout the organization that the company endorsed informal exchanges of knowledge on all types of important business topics, but it also provided them with a methodology for this exchange.

One leader who benefited from this support was Geoff Begg, the vice president and head of acquisition (commercial card) in the Asia Pacific area. Stationed in Sydney and new to American Express back in 2002, Begg found that "integrating [his group] into the larger American Express culture and representing a global value proposition was a daunting task." He said that the networking experience allowed him to share and learn about best practices in other countries, gave him access to senior leaders, and provided a connection to the organization as a whole.

After his initial work with Melissa, Begg and his colleagues in Paris, London, Brazil, and Chicago remained in touch with each other and formed an ad hoc network that facilitated his adaptation to working in an office far removed from headquarters. Because Begg knew that American Express leadership fully endorsed this type of knowledge exchange, he and his colleagues took full advantage of the opportunity to collaborate in this informal network. Through e-mails and telephone calls, they kept each other in the loop about emerging trends and techniques. In many global organizations, it can take days, weeks, or months before such trends and techniques become common knowledge. Begg and his network dramatically reduced the time it took to create this awareness.

As this example suggests, leaders may also participate in the ad hoc groups. They don't necessarily have to participate in any specific leadership role, but as curious parties or potential experts who have a burning interest in, and knowledge about, a key topic. Conversing with the troops has long been a means for leaders to motivate, and wisdom networks are no exception.

In one organization, for instance, more than half of the senior vice presidents were involved in various communities. Many of them noted that their day jobs were fine but filled with administrative work, so the communities gave them a chance to exercise their intellectual muscles and share expertise that they had developed over the years. Because of this high level of leadership involvement, everyone in the company got the message and a number of communities soon evolved into true wisdom networks that quickly added a lot of value to the organization. One community, for instance, formed initially to address diversity issues within the organization. The group quickly came up with some tweaks to the company's diversity policy that the organization incorporated. Encouraged by this success and by the support it received from the company's CEO, the network expanded in terms of both members and scope. In less than a year, it had received the funding and the cooperation from the human resources department to analyze the company's global hiring practices and to address what might be done to increase diversity. Without strong leadership support, this network would not have expanded this quickly.

2. Financial support

Wisdom networks sometimes require a relatively modest sum of money for learning about magnet topics and pilot tests. Linking massive financial investment in major change programs to the development of wisdom networks, however, is strongly discouraged. This type of move will only absorb networks into the organizational structure. Instead, financial support should be provided when networks propose ideas on how to increase their effectiveness or move an innovative idea into a test program or practice. Empowerment is a tremendously strong motivator, and when network participants feel that management is supporting their best ideas with money as well as words, their commitment to networks strengthens.

Making a financial commitment to wisdom networks can help increase their value, but it needs to be done correctly. Done the wrong way, this financial support has a negative impact. Excitement about the financial support triggers initial interest, but it can also create jealousy, disillusionment, disappointment, and discouragement for those networks that don't receive this financial support or as much support as the chosen few. These negative repercussions can diminish creativity within these other networks and may even reduce participation levels.

Yet, there are many ways to help wisdom networks to excel through the judicious use of financial commitment. Budding wisdom networks really don't require a large amount of money, but they do benefit greatly when funds are available for members to participate in things that accelerate the growth of knowledge, such as attending conferences, bringing in experts to make presentations to the group, visiting other companies to see how they're handling related issues, and so on. Therefore, the financial expenditure on networks should be modest—just enough for them to obtain and exchange the necessary knowledge—and, thus, will rarely generate negative repercussions. Given the protests that functional leaders sometimes raise against funding ad hoc groups, it often makes sense to rotate quarterly or yearly funding responsibility for these groups among department heads.

Overcoming the resistance of executives who feel communities of interest can operate just fine without money is more problematic, since they actually can, but they can operate more effectively when they receive some financial support. These resisting executives must understand the business principle of investing to excel at what you do. Networks can be merely good without the investment, but with it they have a much better chance of contributing breakthrough ideas. Just one benchmarking trip to another company may stimulate a line of inquiry that results in a breakthrough.

Perhaps the best argument you can make for funding the development of wisdom networks involves understanding how knowledge grows within them. If you don't spend money to bring in subject-matter experts, to hold company-sponsored knowledge fairs to disseminate wisdom, to stimulate innovation through motivation and excitement, or to create linkages with outside groups, you inadvertently limit the networks' potential benefit to the organization.

This is not to say they won't add value without monetary investment, but by wisely spending money, you may help to bring in fresh perspectives and new sources of knowledge. A financial investment in knowledge fairs or meetings with outside experts, for instance, increases the number of voices being heard within a community. Without this spending, the expert from another company with an original viewpoint would never have a chance to share his or her ideas. A knowledge fair, too, can draw someone out of the shadows who may have something new and important to say, but would never have said it unless stimulated by his or her experience at a knowledge fair. Insights arrive when a wide range of voices are speaking to each other. The friction between these voices often sparks the sort of thinking and discussion that rarely takes place in more homogeneous and well-established groups. As a result, a decent financial investment pays real dividends in wisdom.

3. Facilitation

Helping to catalyze brainstorming sessions, keeping discussions progressing toward a goal, and encouraging participation are all part of this support responsibility. Although facilitators may not be experts in the magnet topic or leaders in the organization, they play a pivotal role by helping talented, strong-minded experts reach closure on topics.

As smart as each individual member of a community may be, groups of experts often lack a skilled professional capable of pulling everything together and turning talk into ideas and ideas into action. Left to their own devices, ad hoc groups can enjoy brilliant exchanges but may never move beyond the brainstorming stage, or may simply jump from one great idea to another with no one to capture them and ensure that any potential benefits are realized from any of them.

Companies are well advised to provide recognized communities with a facilitator, someone who is skilled at moving discussions forward into stages beyond pure brainstorming by using a planned agenda. A facilitator can do everything from resolving conflicts to organizing meetings to filling out paperwork (requests for funding, documenting what took place in a meeting, and so forth).

Facilitators are especially important in diverse networks where people don't always talk the same language. Facilitators can "interpret" both cross-functionally and cross-globally. As you might expect, when very smart people from different backgrounds engage in passionate discussions, things can get heated. Good facilitators can cool the process down when it threatens to get out of hand and can light sparks in lagging conversations that don't seem to be progressing into innovative thinking.

Good facilitation removes the burden of organizing, mediating, and following up. Many members of communities hate these tasks; they joined the communities because they wanted to share information and ideas, not complete paperwork or settle arguments. Facilitators make it much more pleasant for experts to be part of these groups and therefore increase participation.

Companies may choose to find a facilitator within its ranks or go outside for one (usually a consultant). Again, this is a relatively simple form of support than can have a tremendous payoff.

4. Sponsors

Sponsors are organizational leaders who possess budgetary and fiduciary responsibility and believe in wisdom networks. They help procure funds for events, training, or other educational purposes; sponsor knowledge fairs around the magnet topic; and promote the efforts of network champions and their key experts. They also help to secure funding that enables networks to move ideas into the implementation stage.

Sponsors provide financial support, but their role can also include backing specific network initiatives and ideas. They lend both financial and symbolic support to a given community, communicating that they are behind this group and giving them the raised stature that this support implies.

5. Champions

While sponsors offer specific, focused support, champions have a larger role. They support magnet topics with the passion and commitment of an evangelist, and in this evangelical role, they may help convince a sponsor to fund an activity of interest to the wisdom network. Since champions are always leaders, they may also perform a leadership support role, but their mandate is broader. They thoroughly understand a wisdom network's magnet topic and its importance to the organization, and they also communicate its importance to other key people throughout the company. This means they may attempt to persuade management to embrace a recommendation of their wisdom network or they may attempt to recruit other experts for this network. They are the caretakers of the network they are championing and responsible for the network's area of knowledge. Champions may be known by different names, from *knowledge broker* in one organization to *knowledge manager* in another. Whatever the title, it usually conveys that the champion is owner of a certain type of organizational knowledge.

For instance, knowledge managers at the Federal Highways Association (FHWA) champion the cause of tacit knowledge and make sure it is available to those who need it. FHWA has found that the knowledge in people's heads often is more valuable than knowledge captured in writing since the former is constantly being tested and updated through experience in the field. These knowledge managers, then, champion the continuous cataloging and transfer of knowledge from communities within FHWA to those outside of these communities who need the knowledge to do their jobs effectively.

Communities flourish and are increasingly likely to turn into wisdom networks when a knowledge owner or some other leadership figure champions their cause. Unlike sponsorship, this involves a key figure in the company essentially saying, "I believe in what these people are doing and feel that it has tremendous significance for our business." This personal show of support energizes the community and bestows legitimacy on the group to the entire organization. This person needs to explain to management committees, budget control groups, leaders, and supervisors throughout the organization the what, why, when, and how of the emerging wisdom network; in essence, the sponsor becomes the voice of the network to the broader organization.

The champion doesn't need to be a member of the wisdom network, but he or she does need to be a committed, well-informed supporter. The champion's role may involve securing funding; defending members who participate against charges that they are spending too much time on a community project rather than meeting their daily responsibilities; or, conversely, ensuring that those who do participate are not sacrificing their day jobs. The champion may also be the one who recognizes the wise idea that floats out of the group and takes it to an action level, by proposing a project or pilot program to management teams. In all cases, the champion defers credit to the group of experts who form the network, thereby ensuring that wisdom networks do not become mere popularity contests.

6. Technology

Let us begin our technology discussion by focusing on a subtle, support benefit for wisdom networks. Information technology creates an alternative universe in which networks develop ideas with astonishing speed and force. Consider the branding concept of *wikification,* which means the driving of brand development through customer perceptions. Federal Express became "FedEx" because of thousands or even millions of technologically facilitated conversations. The name change came about because customers abbreviated the company name during online exchanges, shortening it because it fit their perception of the company. Federal Express eventually got the message and changed its name accordingly.

Our point is that technology's conversational dynamic provides great support for wisdom networks. Participants can tune in evolving dialogues between customers and other stakeholders to gain information, ideas, and a sense of the changing zeitgeist.

On the less subtle side, technology supports wisdom networks by giving them a better and faster (if not always cheaper) way to communicate. Applications such as the Internet, e-mail, electronic bulletin boards, and virtual meeting rooms facilitate community collaboration. At the same time, this technology can also offer the illusion of support. Something that always sounds promising is to put all content into a single repository. Something that rarely works is to put all content into a single repository and expect that it will change the way information is used, transform into knowledge, and miraculously grow into wisdom. Nifty technology and the promise of superior content work flow are often used in an attempt to pull together scattered pieces of information from all over the company and provide easier access to it. Technology by itself rarely is the answer for solving the problem of scattered intelligence, although it is often misrepresented as such by technology advocates. Technology tends to move information around from here to there, which is not true support for the growth of knowledge, intelligence, and ultimately wisdom.

Technology support for wisdom networks involves providing community members with communication and collaboration tools to make it easier for them to both acquire new knowledge and to share their own. Tools such as virtual desktops, online team work spaces, instant messaging, and voice and video communications are ways to facilitate collaboration with community members in different locations, sometimes in different parts of the world. In some instances, technology support involves online teaching tools that allow communities to spin out information and ideas to interested parties throughout the company.

Technology support may also mean smoothly connecting people in your organization with people in other organizations through sophisticated computer systems. Although conversing with peers within an industry can be a risky proposition, with the right management attention and internally applied expertise, it can often yield great benefits.

Despite all it can do, technology support does not have to be expensive support. In most instances, existing technology could very well be sufficient to help people network more effectively. Too often in companies, however, technology is proprietary to functions, to position levels, or to specific tasks. We're suggesting that companies make these tools available to grassroots communities so they can communicate cross-functionally online or set up collaboration spaces for regular online meetings.

7. Performance reviews

It is important to measure not only how much a company's employees contribute by doing their jobs effectively and meeting their objectives but also how well they exhibit people skills that define a networking organizational culture. These skills include the ability to network with others effectively, teamwork, mentoring, influencing, persuading, and thinking outside the box.

This is probably the trickiest support area both to understand and to implement effectively, in that it means finding rewards for those who participate in and excel at this type of networking activity that do not alienate others. Naturally, such rewards might cause resentment among people, especially if it results in rewards only for those who generate "winning" ideas.

A guiding principle should be that for every ten innovative ideas that emerge, you should expect nine to fail; yet the one that succeeds should more than compensate for the others. To reward only that one is to alienate those who tried, but did not come up with the winning idea. Without all contributors, however, that one successful idea may never have surfaced. The essence of wisdom networks is collaboration, and no action should be taken that discourages these knowledge exchanges.

Therefore, anticipate negative reactions and take steps to minimize their effect. If, for instance, you give spot bonuses only to those who come up with the best ideas in a grassroots group, you're going to engender a lot of grumbling. People will ask, "If Joe got a bonus for his idea in community X, why don't I get a bonus for the idea I came up with in the last meeting of our functional team?"

Factoring both competencies and contributions into performance reviews is a far more effective way to support your communities and increase the odds that they will become wisdom networks. Leaders should be evaluated for their ability to network, mentor, and influence; they should also be evaluated for specific contributions from a job standpoint and to communities. This ensures that people will not be rewarded in an unfair manner or for a single contribution. By communicating that these measures will be used in performance reviews and that everyone has the opportunity to develop networking skills and put them to use, companies diminish protests.

On the positive side, providing increased compensation and promotions to people who excel in unofficial networks encourages greater participation and leadership, which may encourage that expert in the company, who previously had been reluctant to spend much time on community work, to join in. When this expert realizes that the organization is serious about its communities—and nothing communicates this seriousness more than performance review measures—he is much more likely to participate in them.

Perhaps just as significantly, this type of performance review motivates leaders to emerge in various communities. Some people don't take charge until they are in the right situation; they may be experts at their jobs, but they lack the opportunity or the motivation to lead their groups. Communities, on the other hand, present them with level playing fields. Leaders can emerge in communities far more easily than in a more structured environment. To emerge, however, people need to be motivated, and a performance review that esteems community contributions and competencies will achieve this goal.

8. External support

Some companies need outside help to turn their various ad hoc groups into wisdom networks. Support, therefore, involves bringing in outside coaches and consultants. Their role can be systemic or individualized; they can be brought in to design processes and tools that make existing communities more attractive to employees and more efficient in the way they are run. Consultants can help deal with the change management issues that can arise when companies prioritize wisdom networks. They can suggest the best approaches to dealing with people's questions about new performance review measures, for instance, or offer protocols for cross-functional idea sharing.

They may also support leaders who are struggling with the community concept. Some executives may even have difficulty developing the competencies necessary to succeed in a wisdom network environment. They may be mediocre networkers or biased against other functions. Coaching can sometimes help them overcome these obstacles, using 360-degree feedback and other tools to create awareness of why they are not contributing to the new networking paradigm.

Eight-Sided Support at Work

One of UBS's more successful wisdom networks focuses on diversity. It was originally composed of a small group of knowledge owners and experts who came together—figuratively speaking, they often met online—to discuss diversity issues. In many organizations, diversity has become a hot topic, and it's not unusual for task forces and communities to form around this subject. Frequently, however, nothing very substantive or widely implementable comes of these efforts. Although a community may have great discussions and come up with interesting ideas, no real initiatives emerge, and the community fades from the corporate consciousness.

At UBS, though, this ad hoc task force received eight-sided support in the following ways:

1. *Leadership.* The task force was endorsed by management; leaders stepped forward and talked about how important this group's work was to the future of UBS. It was clear to everyone in the organization that the diversity network was doing important work and that its ideas would be listened to.

2. *Financial Support.* The company provided funds for members of this group to attend conferences and visit other companies with innovative diversity initiatives.

3. *Facilitation.* The organization assigned facilitators to the task force, and these facilitators focused on issues such as on-site conferences, which required the scheduling and coordination of numerous speakers.

4. *Sponsors.* A number of knowledge owners took up the task force's diversity cause, helping secure funding and making sure participants had the resources they needed to come up with recommendations.

5. *Champions.* One woman became the spokesperson and clear evangelist for diversity throughout the organization, espousing the virtues of managing with diversity, orienting on educating, mentoring, and recruiting. She became a teacher, custodian, and dispenser of the diversity-related knowledge and accomplishments coming out of the wisdom networks whose magnet topics dealt with diversity.

6. *Technology.* Existing technology was used to keep the group aware of upcoming events and presentations as well to help participants, who were located around the world, keep in touch and make use of virtual meeting spaces.

7. *Performance Reviews.* Management made it clear that leaders who increased organizational value by managing with diversity would be rewarded.

8. *External Support.* Diversity consultants were brought into UBS to share research and also to provide advice on how managing with diversity—and diversity itself within an organization—adds value.

As a result of this support, this task force grew from its informal, temporary status into a full-fledged wisdom network. The diversity wisdom network went on to produce a number of recommendations that were also implemented. The network was so successful that it spun off additional networks, including a women's leadership development network and another for gays, lesbians, bisexuals, and transgendered people. The point to remember is that these positive results occurred because the initial task force received every possible type of support.

Levels of Support: How to Decide Who Gets What

Not only are there eight types of support, but various gradations exist within each. In terms of financial support, an organization can give one community $5,000 to attend outside conferences, while it can spend $100,000 to bring in a consulting firm for another community. If a company identifies fifteen different ad hoc groups and communities, it cannot and should not support each one equally. The company must assess who deserves what based on the topics they are working on and the organization's business priorities.

To begin the assessment, ask yourself the following three questions:

1. How does a given community's topic rate versus other topics being pursued by other communities?

2. Is this group's topic more important to the company's business goals than other groups' topics?

3. If you were to rank this topic versus other topics from a business goal perspective, what number would you assign it?

Based on this assessment, you can make an initial determination of your support level. We have emphasized initial because this determination may change over time. The organization's goals may shift and a given topic may become more or less important. Brilliant ideas may surface from the ad hoc group, and, as a result, management decides that they deserve greater support. It is critical, therefore, to keep asking these three questions regularly, shifting support as the situation dictates. Of course, this doesn't mean giving a great deal of support one moment and withdrawing it at the slightest change in the environment. Rather, organizations should simply give themselves the option of adjusting support levels if major changes occur. Full support of a community may entail providing a significant amount of help in all eight areas. Moderate support might involve mid-level assistance in three or four areas. Light support might mean that leadership endorses a group but does little else.

Be aware, however, that managing this support level does not mean controlling it. You don't want to make communities feel as if you're watching and evaluating their every move. They require and deserve greater freedom than you would give a team that is part of the organizational structure. The whole point of a wisdom network is that it's off the books; you can't find the network on an organizational chart. This is the genius of networks, and why genius can sometimes appear in them.

Determine how much support a given group deserves without intruding on its members. This is not as difficult as it sounds. Asking the three previous questions when you first consider supporting the community usually provides the answer. Later on, you can adjust your support level by evaluating the ideas emerging from each group versus the level of support you're providing. Are the communities where you're providing the most support generating the most wisdom? If so, terrific; if not, you may want to consider adjusting your support model. If one moderately supported ad hoc group is coming up with one terrific idea after another, you might want to increase your help to a higher level.

How to Support Diversity in All Its Forms

Since, as we've said, diverse networks are the wisest networks, organizations should consider this factor when determining their level of support. As a rule, the more diverse a network, the more support it should receive.

To assess the diversity of any community or ad hoc network, you need to consider a number of traits. Obviously, cross-functionality is crucial, but so are a range of ages and experience levels, plus a variety of skills. Ideally, a community will include participants from more than one office; if the firm is international, members should be representative of the company's geographic composition, as well. In certain instances, such as when networks are tackling long-range, industry-impacting topics such as the environment, participants won't be limited to company employees but may also include suppliers, customers, academics, consultants, and competitors.

Remember, the goal of a wisdom network is not reaching consensus as quickly as possible or meeting a short-term goal. Instead, it is to create a brilliant new idea that has a positive impact on a company's business strategy. Homogeneous groups certainly can help further this strategy, but they are unlikely to produce as many breakthrough ideas as heterogeneous groups. When a veteran chemical engineer in Calcutta talks to the young newly hired graduate who has quickly taken on leadership roles within the MIS function, it increases the likelihood of a fresh concept or innovative idea emerging. Support these types of interactions by supporting divergent networks.

One area of difference that is often overlooked is the right brain/left brain mix. Left-brain thinkers are logical and organized; right-brain thinkers are creative and spontaneous. Most people favor either a left-brain or right-brain approach to business issues; however, neither one is better than the other. Some companies, by definition, are more left-brained or right-brained than others. Typically, the more conservative the industry, the more left-brained its company leaders are.

Silicon Valley companies, on the other hand, tend to be filled with right-brain people. Certain functions, too, tend to attract more left- or right-brain thinkers, based on the nature of the work. This is fine, but when it comes to ad hoc networks, you need to strike a balance. The sole function of these networks is idea generation. If you have too much right-brain thinking, you'll have great brainstorming sessions that go nowhere—people are too disorganized, stubborn, and argumentative to focus on and develop the best idea. If you have too much left-brain thinking, innovative ideas and change will gradually diminish, thereby diminishing the overall ROI into your intellectual capital, eventually making your organization less competitive.

A given community has a good mix of left- and right-brain thinking if it exhibits the following wisdom network identity traits:

- The members push the edge of the envelope during discussions, but they are able to bring ideas from the edge and put them through a reality filter before making a recommendation.
- A healthy amount of debate and even conflict arises during verbal and online exchanges, but people are usually able to get past disagreements and identify the best idea.
- Problem-solving approaches run the gamut, with some people favoring radical, high-risk solutions to tough problems while others advocate highly practical, low-risk solutions.
- Some people in a community come up with a hundred ideas in an hour and only one is worth saving, and others come up with only one or two, but 50 percent of their ideas are excellent.
- Some individuals focus on research to address issues, while other participants rely on their own experiences to suggest ways of dealing with a subject.

Obstacles to Obtaining Support—And How to Overcome Them

In the real world, the intention to support ad hoc networks can be thwarted by both people and circumstance. It may be that your organization is in the throes of a crisis and all its attention and energy is focused on dealing with the crisis. As much as it wants to help communities of interest thrive, it is having trouble focusing on supporting them. On the other hand, your company's leadership may not be particularly sophisticated about how to support ad hoc networks to turn them into wisdom networks. Management may substitute a content-management philosophy for true knowledge management and focus on technological support over everything else. In cases like these, you may need to wait for the crisis to pass and the content management approach to fail before your organization can provide the type of support your communities need.

In other instances, though, the problems are more easily and quickly solved. Let's examine three common problems and what to do about them.

1. Community resistance to support

This may seem like a strange problem. Why wouldn't an ad hoc group welcome the tangible and intangible resources a company can provide? The answer goes back to the very reason these communities were first formed. Many times, informal networks emerge because they need to operate outside of the system to get things done. The bureaucratic structures and policies are such that end runs are necessary. People come together in communities because they are frustrated with standard operating procedures or when they feel their job descriptions or status prevents them from following their work passions. So they form informal groups and discover that their information and idea exchanges not only help them do their jobs better but also provide greater job satisfaction because they are exploring subjects and testing ideas that are new, different, and meaningful.

When someone in the community suggests that they might try to obtain leadership endorsement of their efforts or a sponsor, some participants may be aghast. Why spoil a good thing? They like operating underground. They fear that if they become visible, the company will attempt to take over and impose rules and regulations on their thriving network.

What these participants don't realize, however, is that their underground status prevents them from maximizing their value to the company and to themselves. Many ad hoc networks are limited by their invisibility. These networks don't leverage their ideas into other areas of the organization so that the entire company benefits, not just their small group. Because they don't invite a wide range of people into the group to make it as divergent as possible, they don't grow from an ad hoc group into a wisdom network, thereby preventing their expertise from beaming up to higher levels in the organization.

To overcome this problem, an organizational leader must speak to ad hoc group participants, not only communicating these issues but also reassuring the group members that support does not mean interference. Most of the time, when participants realize that they can have their cake and eat it too—that their grassroots networks will continue to function as they did in the past but that they will also receive additional benefits, such as recognition, resources, and rewards—they are happy to accept support.

2. Political agendas

Support should not become political. Unfortunately, some individuals invariably see communities of interest as pieces in a game rather than a way to add organizational value. Don't be surprised, therefore, if an executive decides to throw his weight behind a particular ad hoc group because his top people are members of it or because he thinks he can use it to fulfill his own agenda. In a large manufacturing company, for instance, a vice president decided to champion an ad hoc group that had formed around a new materials technology. The group was composed of an international group of engineers and R&D experts, who were exploring options to the current industry standard.

The company had been reluctant to deviate from the standard, but this group was interested in exploring alternatives, since the material currently used in the manufacturing process had a higher-than-normal defect rate.

The vice president who championed the group had a clear political agenda; he was vying with another vice president for a promotion, and he believed that if the grassroots group came up with a viable option, he would gain an edge over the other vice president. As a result, he not only sponsored the ad hoc network but lobbied hard for financial support as well as for hiring an outside consulting firm to facilitate its efforts. Because he had a good deal of clout, he was able to secure a high level of support.

Politicizing this ad hoc network became an obstacle because other networks were shortchanged. The championed network was receiving support that was disproportionate to what it should have been receiving. Although the network's topic was important, it was not as critical to the business's goals as the topics of some other networks.

Organizations must be vigilant for this type of competitiveness around communities and networks. Wisdom network champions should inform the CEO and other leaders when people start using grassroots groups to further their own agendas. Organizational wisdom should be sacred, off limits to Machiavellian schemes. Unfortunately, too many ambitious executives view organizational knowledge as just one more leverage point to help them get ahead.

3. Overly narrow support

In most companies, more than one grassroots group exists. In companies of significant size, it's not unusual to find ten or more. Sometimes, management is myopic and sees only one of these groups. This may be the result of a political agenda; or, more likely, the cause is human nature. We tend to pay the most attention to the loudest person in the room. If a particular ad hoc network surfaces a particularly compelling idea, it garners the most attention and, therefore, ends up receiving the lion's share of the support.

This may be appropriate if the network's magnet topic exceeds the topics of other groups in importance. Frequently, though, assessment of other groups and their topics doesn't take place. This step is skipped because one ad hoc network has come up with an idea that is the talk of the company; because the members or its champion is a good promoter; or because the idea itself, while less important than some of the others to the company's goals, is glitzier.

As a result, this group receives all eight types of support in large quantities, while the other ad hoc networks are left in the lurch. One group benefits; the rest are demoralized. The funneling of resources and other forms of support to one group tells the others that they aren't important, which, in turn, causes them to lose energy and enthusiasm.

To secure business-appropriate support, companies must resist the temptation to skip the assessment step. This means that a leader in the organization has to step up and insist on this assessment before one group is anointed the company's star ad hoc network. If business priorities justify the anointment, that is great. A little due diligence, on the other hand, can save a company from misallocating its resources.

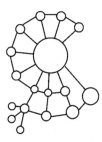

CHAPTER 6

Step 4: Boundary Crossing and Role Breaking—Ensure Diverse Perspectives

Although boundaries and roles are necessary for getting work done, they also can block a free-flowing exchange of information and ideas. Structure naturally dictates that certain people should do X but not Y in order to maximize performance. Based on your job description and place in the hierarchy, you have both vertical (authority) and horizontal (function) parameters that define what you do. These parameters create order and increase efficiency. Unfortunately, they also make it difficult—if not impossible—for ad hoc groups to become wisdom networks. On the other hand, as organizations become flatter and traditional boundaries and roles break down, they tend to be less effectively innovative. Although they may come up with more creative ideas because of the participatory culture, they will often struggle to implement these ideas. Therefore, hierarchical structures where everyone has an assigned role and task make implementation easier.

Still, the diverse people and ideas that fuel wisdom networks don't emerge when boundaries and roles are too religiously observed. As brilliant as any group of people might be, if they represent the same function, managerial level, race, gender, and age, they will rarely produce anything approaching wisdom. They may be highly competent, but they will lack the diverse perspectives, information, and experiences that yield innovative, breakthrough ideas.

For this reason, organizations need to encourage boundary crossing and role breaking. This can be a challenge, because boundaries and roles exert a strong hold on people, especially in conservative, tightly structured companies. We'll suggest ways to meet this challenge, starting with an exploration of the myriad boundaries and roles that exist in any organization.

Lines That Must Be Crossed

There are more boundaries and roles than you might expect. Lets look at the most common ones and the reasons why people are reluctant to cross them:

1. Functional boundaries

This is the most obvious type of boundary. Despite the existence of cross-functional teams, organizations still have taboos against people becoming involved in projects outside their functions. Companies often don't want their marketing people making suggestions for improving the payroll system or their MIS experts coming up with new ad slogans. The rationale behind the taboo seems to be "Don't step on the other person's toes; they know a lot more about the subject than you do." We're not suggesting that it would be beneficial for an MIS person to usurp a marketing person's responsibilities, but we are suggesting that a dialogue between people from these functions might produce a fresh and potentially useful perspective.

In the real world, however, organizations often don't acknowledge that cross-functional dialogue occurs constantly, especially in the hidden networks within a company. There is a need for more of these dialogues, and a need for organizations to encourage them. Many key business issues are relevant to people in all functions. Everyone may be trying to reduce costs, for instance, or attempting to figure out a better way to develop their younger people into managers and leaders. One functional expert may have a brilliant approach to a shared issue, but others will never learn of it unless networks encourage boundary crossing.

2. Hierarchical boundaries

In a large company, people typically interact within their structural layers—for example, middle managers talk to middle managers, senior leaders talk to senior leaders, and so on. Again, this is logical, because people at the same level have similar concerns and issues. Despite the move away from a military structure, however, fraternization between privates and generals is frowned upon. Wariness exists between levels—a feeling that senior people cannot possibly relate to what junior people are experiencing (and vice versa).

When ideas are locked in a given level, however, they lack richness; they don't take into account the perspective of someone high up in the organization, someone in the middle, and someone just starting out. Wisdom networks need the participation of experts with a full range of titles; expertise is not the province of just the top people.

3. External boundaries

While partnering with suppliers and even competitors on joint projects has become more common than in the past, organizations still view these collaborations as being special circumstances. Typically, they occur in pursuit of a specific goal—for example, an industry-wide research project to find a better product material. Ad hoc networks exchanging information and ideas with outside organizations strike many companies as anathema, especially when the exchange takes place largely unsupervised.

4. Diversity-related boundaries

As much as organizations promote diversity, individuals often are naturally reluctant to respond to these initiatives. Having spent years in an old boys' network, veteran leaders may be reluctant to share their thoughts with young women. Age, gender, race, nationality, and other differentiating traits often form unconscious boundaries in organizations.

Most people do not consciously discriminate or are even aware that they tend to gravitate toward groups of their own kind; however, think about the hidden networks in your organization. The odds are that one group consists of young, male techies; another group involves middle-aged women; a third group is made up of veteran employees. Naturally, these groups are somewhat homogeneous because of their topics—a women's leadership group is going to be composed of women—but it should not be restricted to women if you are attempting to transform it into a wisdom network. Magnet business topics benefit from a network of diverse participants, and if these networks are overly homogeneous, they will likely address topics myopically.

We are not advocating boundary crossing for boundary crossing's sake. It is neither a panacea for a lack of innovation nor a guarantee of effective implementation. Therefore, the key is for organizations to communicate that communities and networks are open to everyone, and that crossing boundaries within the context of these communities, at least, is appropriate behavior.

Larry Mohl is vice president and chief learning officer for Children's Healthcare of Atlanta, a pediatric hospital system that has received many accolades for its quality of care. Contributing to its success has been its ability to provide a structure and culture for various healthcare providers to share best practices across traditional boundaries. Traditionally in hospitals, there's a diverse care-provider team—medical residents, veteran nurses, first-year nurses, physicians with different areas of specialization, and so on. Although everyone works together to help patients, they may lack the inclination, time, or opportunity to capture the knowledge they share with one another in a way that results in sustained changed practice.

Children's has encouraged knowledge sharing in many ways, including supporting networks that have formed around specific diseases. Talking about the success the hospital has had with a network that focuses on asthma, Mohl notes that:

> [T]here are bad things, good things, and best things you can do for patients. We want to adopt the best practices. This requires a combination of evaluating the research and sharing what the nurses know,

what the clinicians know, and what the doctors—across all the practices—know. There are numerous areas where we are supporting networks across discipline practices. A physicians' practice council provides a system to manage exchanging the benefits from each network. Physicians, nurses, and other clinicians are motivated to participate in the networks by their commitment to improving healthcare for children.

Encouraging healthcare professionals to cross boundaries for a cause about which they are passionate is similar to encouraging business professionals to cross boundaries on a magnet topic about which they are vitally interested. With proper encouragement from leaders and an informal network where they feel free to communicate with people outside their usual frame of reference, experts will be more than willing to share ideas and information that they would otherwise keep confined to a small group.

How to Encourage Courage

No question, it takes some real daring to cross a clearly delineated boundary, to transcend a well-defined role, or to stand up to typically vocal naysayers to any new idea or hint of change. Organizational leaders, though, can do a lot to help people to find their valor and to encourage them to act upon their thoughts.

Specifically, they should consider the benefits of taking the following steps:

1. Validate networks as an alternative corporate universe

People need to understand that the world of communities and networks forms an alternative universe within their organizations where some of the ordinary rules of corporate life don't apply, and that this alternative world is no threat to their security or ability to succeed in their jobs.

Leaders can validate the existence of networks by acknowledging the hidden networks and the unacknowledged experts within their organizations. They must bring community activities and ideas into the corporate consciousness.

By making the invisible visible—that is, by using both written and verbal communication tools to create awareness about these ad hoc groups—companies can encourage participation from all organizational levels, across all functional areas of responsibility, and, perhaps most telling, from a highly diverse community of employees.

When leaders use formal communication as well as informal conversation to acknowledge and approve of communities, the word quickly spreads. Once a community composed of individuals from different departments and different levels is recognized, people are much more likely to look for a topic of interest that excites them. As they get excited about such topics and interests, it helps them to overcome their fear of stepping over a line, or standing up to a naysayer's objections.

Instead of thinking to themselves, "That's outside my area of responsibility," they realize that in this alternative—but very real—universe, some formal areas of responsibility are less important than passion for and knowledge about a given topic.

2. Endorse pioneering

Leaders need to do more than just encourage people to join existing communities, they need to make their people understand that it is not only acceptable but advisable to form new ones. If the environment is receptive, experts will naturally form groups designed to complete end runs around the bureaucracy, to test daring new concepts, and to figure out time-saving ways of getting things done.

At UBS, for example, the company has become so large that setting up a desk, computer, and telephone system for a new employee can be a time-consuming process. There is often paperwork to fill out for each new hire, security processes to work through, system logins and passwords to set up, supplies to pull together from various departments, and a training process that is designed to get new people up to speed rapidly on all aspects of compliance. Combined, these tasks were often quite laborious.

A mid-level executive in a key UBS office became frustrated with the time it took to get a new employee fully functional. She decided that there had to be a faster way for new employees to get through the initial routines required to start being productive, other than by following the existing standard procedures of each group separately. She brought together a loosely knit group of people from each area to try and expedite the process. Because she had been with the company for some time and possessed strong contacts—with a tremendous amount of understanding of the core processes in how to get such things done—in many functions, she and her ad hoc network were able to develop a system that decreased the setup time and significantly shortened the learning curve for new staff.

One of their innovations, for instance, was reversing the typical order of steps needed to set up an office. Instead of doing the paperwork first and having to await results from each submission, they switched the order so that while the paperwork was submitted and being reviewed, temporary arrangements were made so that the new people were able to start work and be productive right away. One of their first tasks was helping to complete the remaining paperwork to keep track of recently hired staff, to specify their preferences in supplies, and to register for online training and education courses. The new employees themselves helped to shorten the new-joiner process by getting things done on their own without having to wait on extremely busy individuals in many different areas to get their information through various processes.

The manager recognized that UBS endorsed this type of pioneering effort, which required the active participation of different functions to make her alternative process work. She shared her success with her management peers in other departments, and ultimately processes were changed to take advantage of her innovation. It's possible that, without UBS's endorsement of such innovative actions, she might have implemented her shortcut but kept the results of her pioneering effort to herself. She and her group would have benefited, but no one else in the company would have, thereby minimizing the value of her wisdom rather than maximizing it.

3. Accept boundary crossing in the shadows

Sometimes organizations need to proceed slowly because significant resistance exists to boundary crossing or role breaking. In these cases, leaders need to recognize this fact and encourage people to work with other functions, levels, types of people, or outsiders removed from the spotlight.

Typically, what happens is that boundary-crossing ad hoc groups form, they work on a project about which they are passionate, come up with new ideas and approaches, and, at some point, their concepts dovetail perfectly with what the company needs.

One large, tradition-bound food product organization had a strong identity in the marketplace. A small group of people within this company, however, was dissatisfied with the way the company's brand was perceived, so they began researching how tradition-heavy companies such as theirs remade their brands effectively. A few members of the marketing department were members of this community, but it also consisted of people from MIS, manufacturing, and human resources. Some members were higher-level executives, but middle managers and relative newcomers to the company also joined the community. They began networking with a consultant whose expertise was branding. It took almost two years, but in that time, market share was starting to fall, competitive threats had grown more serious, and the CEO was finally ready to listen to new branding approaches. Because this community had done its homework, it was embraced by the CEO, demonstrating to everyone in the company that boundary crossing within these networks was fine.

DaimlerChrysler is an organization that has done a terrific job encouraging people to cross boundaries. Ever since a 1996 knowledge-sharing forum held in conjunction with accounting firm Ernst & Young, Daimler-Chrysler's leaders have encouraged employees to cross all structurally imposed boundaries and come together in communities to pursue key business topics, resulting in the creation of between two hundred and three hundred dynamically evolving communities.

Although DaimlerChrysler used cross-functional teams for end-to-end vehicle production, which reduced the amount of rework that occurred with traditional linear teams, the company found that its cross-functional nature actually separated experts in a given area from one another.

In the old linear system, for instance, brake system experts for small cars would work with brake system experts for large cars, and this fostered a natural knowledge exchange and allowed veteran employees to assume mentoring roles. The cross-functional system ironically created new boundaries that were difficult to cross in this structure. Because these teams were effective, the company didn't want to disband them or go back to the linear approach.

Therefore, DaimlerChrysler leadership encouraged the creation of a system of communities, ad hoc groups that would allow specialists to cross newly created boundaries in order to exchange knowledge with other experts in their area, albeit ones who had more or less experience or different types of knowledge within a general area. These communities, known as tech clubs, became responsible for managing organizational knowledge within a given technical area. As part of this responsibility, people could communicate with fellow specialists whom they might not otherwise communicate with in the cross-functional system.

In a very significant way, DaimlerChrysler has taken to heart step one: Validate networks as an alternative corporate universe. With two hundred to three hundred communities of people crossing every conceivable boundary, they have created an extremely large alternative universe.

Politically Wise Strategies: How to Avoid Stepping on Powerful People's Toes

Although some companies are more enlightened about boundary crossing and role breaking than others, most offer some resistance for one or more of the reasons we've discussed. In addition, some leaders see role breaking and boundary crossing as dangerous pursuits. They are philosophically opposed to them, believing that they endanger the inherent order of an organization. Other highly politicized executives oppose boundary crossing on territorial grounds because they view these crossings as a diminution of their power.

In hidden networks, boundary crossing and role breaking occur behind the scenes. When these networks start to surface—that is, when their contributions are acknowledged and their ideas are talked about and implemented—the networks face resistance, and that resistance tends to increase when organizations provide cash rewards to network stars.

Rewards can have both negative and positive effects. In this case, rewards not only draw everyone's attention to the boundary crossing and role breaking that has occurred, but they inflate egos, thereby creating tensions with those who were not similarly rewarded and generating complaints that often draw the complainers' bosses into the fray. These bosses, in turn, suggest it might not be a good idea to reward people for working outside their assigned roles.

If you want to decrease resistance to these necessary boundary crossings, don't give cash rewards. Instead consider creating a pilot test to demonstrate that boundary crossing and role breaking in networks do not just benefit the networks but add value to the organization and its functions. Typically, support for boundary-crossing behaviors increases after a successful pilot test, when everyone has tangible evidence of the benefits.

As a community of interest or a community of practice evolves in the value it generates and becomes a true wisdom network—or as any grassroots group evolves into a more established entity working on a key business topic—the individual members bring skills and knowledge back to their regular jobs. Through their participation in a vibrant community, they gain insights about key business topics. They acquire new knowledge and skills that often make them more effective in their jobs. They also acquire new contacts that can help their work teams accomplish their objectives. If their wisdom network is successful and praised by management, their participation reflects well on their bosses. All this makes company leaders more willing to permit the boundary crossing that is critical to wisdom networks.

When organizations are embarking on major change programs, people who participate in ad hoc groups and communities often become leaders and facilitators of change initiatives, precisely because of their boundary-crossing, role-breaking experiences. By participating in these networks, they have learned how to form alliances with a diverse group of people and work outside of the traditional boundaries.

Change initiatives often require people who can break away from the traditional way of doing things and embrace alternative approaches. Perhaps even more significantly, participating in wisdom networks increases an individual's adaptability. As part of these networks, people must be flexible as they test new ideas and risk-taking concepts. When one approach is not working, they learn how to tolerate greater degrees of risk and to change direction. This flexibility is essential for change programs, and a company's leaders appreciate the boundary-crossing, role-breaking flexibility people develop as part of wisdom networks.

Allowing a wisdom network to prove its worth, therefore, is a good strategy to melt resistance to boundary crossing, but it also takes time. In the interim, you might also consider noting the points of resistance and steering around them. In most instances, organizations have several magnet business topics that draw people into hidden networks. You need to be cognizant of which ones, when they surface, might cause certain executives in your company to get their noses out of joint.

Politically astute leaders often avoid confrontations by choosing the right time to surface the ideas and recommendations of a particular network. Certain areas are touchy, and it makes no sense to plunge forward if you know that a powerful leader in the company will blow his or her top upon learning that people are violating the company's structure and assigned roles.

In time, and with the success of other wisdom networks, these individuals will usually become more accepting of people taking on other roles and crossing dividing lines. In the interim, though, they should remain in the shadows until a more propitious time.

In most cases, individuals will also seek the path of least resistance when they create ad hoc groups that cross boundaries. Jenny, for instance, was a young, lower-level marketing manager in a branch office working for a large, multinational corporation. Jenny had become increasingly disturbed by the disconnect between customers and the organization. In her marketing job, she had witnessed a growing gap between the company's branding strategy and the real concerns of customers. She knew that customers had complained for years about the company's slow response to requests for changes in customer service policies, information dissemination, and billing procedures. Jenny was also aware that the salespeople were too focused on finding and converting new prospects so that current customer concerns were a secondary priority.

At first, Jenny tried to organize salespeople into an ad hoc group around the topic of customer service, but the head of the sales department got wind of it and discouraged his people from joining the group. He thought Jenny, as a marketing manager, was trying to usurp his authority, although this was the furthest thing from her mind.

Jenny persevered; she shifted her approach and reformulated the community around wider-ranging customer issues and drew a cross section of functions, job levels, and ages to the community. She also established links with outside sources, including consulting groups and industry trade organizations, that could provide insight into how other companies were dealing effectively with a wide swath of customer concerns. After visits to other companies and a series of meetings, Jenny's group presented its champion—one of the top executives in the company—with some of the group's conclusions about how to improve customer relationships. This executive in turn presented the findings to the CEO, who was so impressed with their efforts that he created a special customer issues position and asked Jenny to pursue it full-time.

Fostering Collaboration, Not Conflict

One potential repercussion of encouraging boundary crossing and role breaking is tension among network members. When people feel passionate about a topic and are willing to move outside of their usual job responsibilities to address it, they may come into conflict with other members of a community or network. Remember, these communities are not hand-picked to ensure compatibility. They are composed of very smart people with strongly held opinions. When they come together, intellectual sparks fly because of their high degree of commitment and expertise.

The possible downside, of course, is that other community members may resent a particular individual's way of crossing a boundary. They may feel one person lacks the experience necessary to cross that boundary or that another person is out of line because he or she has taken on a role that seems inappropriate. When an MIS community member espouses a provocative position on hiring protocols, for instance, a community member from human resources may be tempted to respond, "You don't know what you're talking about!" Operating tangential to the organizational structure, communities lack the traditional processes and policies that help get work done. At such times, community or network leaders must step forward and do everything possible to manage conflict and push for consensus.

To do so, community roles must be assumed. Although people need to transcend their hierarchical roles to an extent, they must also find new roles within these ad hoc groups. This isn't as critical in ad hoc groups as they are in communities of interest, which are not as critical as roles in communities of practice. However, as grassroots groups become increasingly tied in to major business goals, roles become one way of moving group members toward consensus and keeping them highly productive. We have found that communities without roles tend to maintain a debate team ambience. People exchange stimulating ideas and have thought-provoking discussions, but the conversation doesn't move forward toward recommendations and plans, and ultimately into action.

You may have read the case history about Xerox in 1977. To stay on top of its market, the company needed to reinvent itself, so it created a brainstorming team consisting of some of the best and brightest minds in the company. Boundaries were crossed, roles were broken, and the team came up with tremendous ideas for new products. One of these ideas, in fact, was for a personal computer. Xerox, ironically, failed to capture the value from these ideas and, of course, we all know the success of IBM today.

Many reasons exist for this failure, but we suspect one major factor involved a lack of clear roles. When teams fail to capitalize on their considerable expertise, the absence of roles is often to blame. Unfettered creativity sounds good in theory, but, in practice, it needs to be balanced with methodology and objectives. When people take on key roles—such as leader, facilitator, administrator, researcher, or sponsor—the group is much more likely to move toward a goal. Wisdom networks not only create great ideas but also are skilled at moving from a discussion of these ideas to consensus around the best one. Strong collaborative efforts help to move ideas up and out into the organization. When everyone in a community is behind an idea 100 percent, it gathers force and is presented in a way that is far more powerful than if the group is split on which idea is best.

Therefore, it is important for a group to adopt clear roles. Someone needs to step up and assume leadership. Another person has to be responsible for obtaining necessary resources for the group. A third must keep a record of the group's discussions and decisions. These roles make it far easier for a group of very smart people who have moved beyond their traditional roles and boundaries to use their knowledge for a distinct purpose.

Members of a community or network should also adopt certain principles or guidelines that will help them to transcend their differences and get things done. Many members of a new community are operating in unexplored territory. They have crossed functional boundaries or transcended traditional roles, and, as a result, they lack an established method for getting work done. Establishing norms about how to resolve disagreements, how often to meet, what the community's purpose is, and so on will make it easier to keep the group moving forward toward its goal.

The Business Benefit: Breakthrough Solutions

With all this talk of crossing boundaries, the question becomes how specifically does an organization benefit? What magic occurs when people ignore the lines that divide them from other functions or when they take on issues that they would not ordinarily approach? The magic isn't limited to so-called great ideas. Not to be cynical about it, but great ideas are a dime a dozen. Wisdom networks produce ideas that cut costs, improve operating efficiencies, take advantage of new market opportunities, and so on. They aren't great ideas just in *theory*, but in practice.

Too often, when companies get stuck or are facing a difficult problem, they bring in an expensive team of consultants to find solutions. We have nothing against consultants, but many times, the answers reside within a company rather than outside of it. Perhaps you have heard the expression that people use only 5 percent of their brains. Well then, organizations use only 5 percent of their wisdom. When people depart from their roles and move across boundaries in pursuit of a topic of interest, a greater percentage of this wisdom is released for use. When they are excited about what they're working on and they are able to look at the topic without the limits imposed by their job responsibilities or decision-making level, they often have the energy and the freedom necessary to find breakthrough solutions.

If you were to observe people in a wisdom network working on a specific issue, you would see that their approach varies from that of a typical team, and this difference owes a lot to their ability to get past traditional boundaries and roles. Specifically, people in wisdom networks:

1. Challenge the conventional wisdom

People in wisdom networks don't feel they must adhere to their function's or even their boss's way of seeing things associated with the magnet topic. Within the egalitarian environment of a wisdom network, they don't feel constrained by how they "should" look at a problem. Many times, they will contact outside experts and receive data or opinions that force them to question standard operating procedures.

2. Explore "what if" scenarios

Often, the "what if" scenarios require revamping traditional functional or departmental roles.

- What if manufacturing and marketing collaborated on the new design process software?
- What if we were a small company scratching for survival and needed to scrap our old, ineffective distribution strategy and come up with a new one in a week?
- What if we shared with customers financial information that would help them understand how we charge them?

You can't ask these what if questions if you are limited by your job responsibilities and the chain of command.

3. Propose bias-free solutions or strategies

Frequently, organizational ideas are biased in favor of functions or hierarchical levels. Although these biases may be hidden, many executives look out for their own people or propose programs that will make them look good. In wisdom networks, the absence of traditional boundaries and roles and the creation of new roles within the network takes politics and game playing out of the equation. The primary motivation is to share expertise and to demonstrate a new way to achieve a goal or solve a problem.

To illustrate the benefits of these three differentiators, consider how a UBS wisdom network addressed a foreign exchange (FX) currency global business issue. At the time, this business was highly ranked but not number one, and this network of business experts wanted to explore how UBS might increase its business with international clients around trading currencies.

After much discussion, the network's members came up with a technology solution requiring multifunctional, collaborative technology tools and cross-functional communication. They had the radical idea that if UBS created an instant messaging channel to its international clients—a channel that hooked UBS research analysts, settlement professionals, risk managers, and others together—they could answer client questions or offer advice with greater speed and efficiency than any system that was currently in place in the industry.

In 2000, they wanted to pilot test this idea. Getting all these different functions to participate in this pilot test required a huge range of people to cross boundaries. People who never talked directly to clients had to take on this new responsibility, albeit with some preparatory training.

The results were beyond the expectations of even the wisdom network. Clients found it incredibly useful to receive near real-time research about how changing country conditions affected currency markets. Once they received this information, clients appreciated having immediate, online access to analysts who could offer advice. Ultimately, this pilot test transformed UBS's business model and helped UBS become the number one FX house in the world for the past three years.

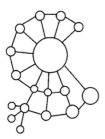

CHAPTER 7

Step 5: Hide-and-Seek—
Identify the Experts

In small organizations, everyone knows who the experts are. Ask any manager whom she or he turns to when a particularly sticky problem arises or whom everyone asks for advice when a challenging project is assigned, and this manager will immediately name one or two people.

Experts, however, often become lost in midsize or large organizations. Although they are known to their bosses and their immediate colleagues, these experts often exist in de facto isolation. They may be highly selective in their interactions with people in other functions, and the company's leaders in general aren't aware of them.

As we've seen, when experts don't interact cross-functionally, organizations fail to maximize the value of their expertise for major business initiatives. And when they don't share their information and perspectives with each other, creative synergies fail to emerge. When leaders are unaware of who in their organizations are the real experts, these people essentially are untapped resources because they are not included on teams and task forces where their expertise could be vital to successful outcomes.

Ad hoc groups offer organizations a way around these problems. In any community in any company, you will find experts involved in wide-

ranging, free-flowing discussions that transcend function and focus on issues. This is great, but for wisdom networks to form and function at peak
capacity, companies must identify experts who are well versed in magnet
business topics. By paying attention to what is going on in communities
and by talking to managers about who the real pros are, organizations can
identify subject matter experts and take full advantage of their value to the
organization.

The Four-Step Identification Process

In any organization, all types of experts exist. For example, you can find
people who have mastered the intricacies of the accounting system and
individuals who are brilliant when it comes to repairing equipment. There
are experts in legal areas pertaining to contracts and those who are skilled
in training. The list is almost endless. Entire recruiting campaigns might
have been directed at bringing in a particular type of expertise.

All these experts are important, but a wisdom network requires experts
who possess subject matter knowledge in areas central to key business
topics as well as collaborating, mentoring, and other related competencies.
More esoteric knowledge (accounting system intricacies) and specific skills
(training) are obviously significant, but the individuals who know a lot
about issues critical to the company's business goals are the ones who must
be spotlighted.

First, companies need an expert identifier, someone who knows experts when he or she sees them, can bring them out of the hidden shadows,
and can enable them to connect with others. This identifier must be an
individual who has a great grasp of how the company works. Take, for
example, Euan Semple, appointed as head of KM solutions at the BBC.
According to a June 2005 interview in *Inside Knowledge* ("The Knowledge:
Euan Semple," by Sandra Higgison, available at www.ikmagazine.com),
Semple maintained a database of who at the BBC was interested in what,
eventually leveraging his expertise to catalyze social interaction across the
organization, helping people to connect where interests dovetailed and
form communities of interest. By supporting various emerging collaborative technologies such as bulletin boards, blogs, wikis, and twikis, Semple

did not aggressively advocate these technologies but merely made them available and encouraged their use. In a short time, many staff took advantage of them and some very visible communities emerged around various topics.

Finding a person in your organization like Semple to champion expert identification/connection efforts, therefore, should be a top priority. Although the means may vary from company to company, the goal always relates to the following question: Who are the experts in my company and how do we bring them out?

Once this identifier is in place, the organization is ready to engage in the following four-step process:

Step #1. Find who has subject matter expertise related to your organization's business goals. This isn't difficult, because you can ask line managers in appropriate areas the following questions:

- Whom do you turn to when you're facing a particularly difficult or vexing problem?
- Who knows more about X (subject) than anyone else in your group?
- Whom do others in your group seek out when they are having difficulty or need assistance with a challenging project?

Step #2. Being a subject matter expert in a key area is only the first qualification. Some subject matter experts may know a great deal, but they may not be willing to share what they know or adept at sharing it. Therefore, Step #2 is to determine which experts are also good communicators and teachers. Just because you are extraordinarily knowledgeable about a subject doesn't automatically mean you can communicate it to others even if you would like to. On the other hand, there are those who enjoy mentoring and offering insights and inside information about best practices to colleagues and others with less experience.

Step #3. Figure out which of these people are active participants in communities and other ad hoc groups (just because you belong to a community doesn't mean you're fully engaged in it). Some experts are functional-minded and aren't interested in sharing their knowledge with people outside of their function. Others just aren't aware of the communities or aren't motivated to join them. The exceptional experts are those who relish the exchange of ideas that occurs in these groups. They seize the chance to exchange information and perspectives with a diverse group of people, to debate hot button issues, and to create new approaches with other experts. This step involves finding those individuals who are fully engaged.

Step #4. Identify the experts who are also leaders. Certain experts are more than just active community participants. They are catalysts and resource providers. These experts/leaders challenge other people in their networks to come up with new and better ideas. They make an effort to secure additional information that the network requires or to recruit new members. In addition, they are able to take a network's idea and push it up to decision makers.

All people identified in each of the four steps are valuable to wisdom networks. At each step, though, you ratchet up the value of the individual. The experts/leaders are worth their weight in gold. They often champion the causes of networks, pushing great ideas into real projects and programs.

Different organizations have their own identification processes that may not follow this four-step process exactly, but they produce the same effect. BP Amoco, for instance, has a project called BP Connect designed to create an internal Yellow Pages directory of experts in the organization. The company compiled a list of its own known experts and also requested employees with expertise to list themselves. In this way, the company made it easy for people to know whom to contact when they needed help in a specific area. In the first year alone, ten thousand employees used this system. Perhaps even more significant, this directory of experts allowed leadership to figure out who in the company was expert in what. Certainly, a functional head knew who the experts in his or her function were, but in a company as large as BP Amoco, those functional heads probably didn't know who the experts were in other functions. In addition, this identification process stimulated the formation of ad hoc networks because it also created awareness among all experts (no matter what their place in the hierarchy was) who their fellow experts were.

When organizations are adept at identifying experts, they have the opportunity to maximize the wisdom contained in their organizations. Let us look at the specific benefits that accrue to companies where the experts are known to many, if not all.

The Advantages of Identifying the Experts

Organizations that identify the subject matter experts who contribute their knowledge consistently and effectively benefit in many ways. Even if their identification is limited to Step #1, they realize the following benefits:

1. Synergistic exchanges across functions that produce wisdom

When you know who the subject matter experts in key business topics are, you are in a much better position to help them share their expertise with the right people. You can encourage networks of complementary experts. In other words, one expert in sales to international customers may have no interaction with an expert in sales to domestic customers. In the normal course of their jobs, little common ground exists—their customers have very different needs and operate in very different environments. At the same time, however, both experts possess strong perspectives and knowledge about customer service. If they began meeting and talking about hot-button business issues related to customer service, they might hit upon a better way of managing the process. In other words, one's knowledge supplements the other type of knowledge.

When a company's leadership is aware of who the key subject experts are, it can ensure that these individuals are part of more formalized networks that arise in response to specific problems or opportunities. Top people can impress upon these experts how important their contributions are, and how crucial their membership in diverse networks is.

In one large high-tech company, management identified forty subject matter experts in areas critical to the company's success and encouraged their participation in various ad hoc groups. One of these groups involved branding strategies, a key area for the company because it felt that the marketplace's perception of the company was fuzzy at best and that it was hurting the company's overall performance.

Although this particular network included marketing experts, several experts from other functions also participated. One of them was the company's top software designer, a brilliant man who liked nothing better than spending all his time immersed in design work. Once management identified him as an expert and communicated the importance of sharing his knowledge with others, he was willing to join this emerging network. Unlike some of the other participants, he believed that most customers didn't realize that their software products were more intelligently designed than those of the company's competitors. In one of the network discussions, he responded to a marketing expert's challenge to define what he meant by *intelligent*. At first, the marketer was unable to understand what the software designer was saying—they spoke two very different languages—and kept pushing the software designer to clarify his explanations. The software guy pushed back, challenging the marketing person to justify the current branding approach. By pushing each other, they both gained a fresh perspective, and what resulted was a branding approach that captured the elegance of product design and communicated it in an accessible way.

2. Ferreting out future leaders

The process of identifying subject matter experts also provides organizations with a way to spot undiscovered leaders. At least some of these subject matter experts also meet the criteria outlined in Steps #2, #3, and #4. Because they have been so involved in their particular area of expertise, they may not have attracted notice as potential leaders beyond their small circle. The identification process, therefore, helps certain people, who might otherwise have remained in the shadows, step into the spotlight. Of course, some of them are perfectly content to remain in the shadows; they have no interest in leadership positions. This is fine, since some people are better suited to the roles of subject matter experts. On the other hand, individuals who have great subject matter knowledge and leadership qualities are tremendously valuable and need to be identified and placed on leadership tracks.

3. Retaining top people

Identification is its own reward. Letting people know that the company's leadership respects their expertise and wants to put them in the best position possible to share it with others provides positive reinforcement. Experts are in short supply and high demand. If their expertise is largely unacknowledged, they are more likely to look for jobs where they can receive greater recognition. By identifying them as being in an elite group, these subject matter experts often feel empowered and appreciated.

You've Identified the Experts, Now What?

Once organizations know who their subject matter experts are, they need to create pathways for these experts to share their knowledge at the right time and in the right place. As we've discussed, companies with cultures receptive to networking are usually better able to maximize the value of their identified experts than less-network-friendly organizations. Realistically, however, most organizations can do a better job of steering their experts into the right groups so that they contribute consistently and effectively to important business goals.

Typically, network-minded companies identify subject matter experts and awareness of these experts spreads quickly. For instance, a sales manager in the Dallas office of a global company is talking with a major customer who explains his interest in investing in a Pan-Asian group of companies. The sales manager is aware that the CFO of the Tokyo office is an expert in this area, and he calls and requests assistance. The Tokyo expert says it sounds like an interesting opportunity and asks the Dallas sales manager to e-mail him information about the customer and other aspects of the prospective deal. The sales manager does so, but he receives relatively little feedback—a perfunctory note and nothing else.

Clearly, the Tokyo expert is wary because the Dallas sales manager has breached protocol. Although he might be responsive if the Dallas manager had asked for sales figures related to his product area, a request about foreign investments seems odds to the CFO in Tokyo; he is not accustomed to sales managers from the United States asking him about investment issues in Japan. He sees no direct benefit for his office or the company in providing the information the sales manager seeks, and he is uncomfortable sharing such information in a way he has never done before.

Variations on this theme occur frequently after experts become well-known to people outside of their function. As we've discussed, they may resist sharing information for numerous reasons, including:

- Concern they will be inundated with queries and become overwhelmed with requests for assistance, not having sufficient time to complete their own assignments.
- Suspicion that they might get into political hot water by giving information to individuals of whom their boss may not approve.
- Fear that by giving away information and ideas, their position will be diminished; that their knowledge is what makes them valuable, and the more they give away, the less valuable they are perceived to be and the less they will be paid for their work.
- Misunderstandings between people who aren't able to communicate effectively together. Misunderstandings occur frequently because protocols on how to do everything from holding meetings to entertaining clients to soliciting advice vary from one country to the next. As a result, an expert in Country A may be unwilling to share his knowledge with a colleague in Country B because he has been offended. He may also resist sharing what he knows because in his country, knowledge is exchanged only vertically, and in the other country, horizontal exchanges are also a norm.

There are several ways to overcome all these types of resistance. First, companies must develop pathways linking disparate individuals that offer alternative ways for people to find, communicate, and establish relationships with them. In other words, they should provide access to experts in ways that go beyond standard operating procedures. In many companies, the process of requesting help from an expert requires going through the expert's boss and that boss's boss. It may also involve delays between the time a request is made and when help is received—with other matters frequently taking priority.

Myrtis Meyers, director of research and planning at YMCA-USA, is attempting to provide greater access to experts, based on her belief that some of the best knowledge exists deeply embedded in the experiences of individual staff from separate and distinct Y locations. For this reason, leveraging that expertise from one Y branch to another is one of her top goals. To establish the pathways between experts at each Y might appear to be a daunting task given the thousands of Y locations, yet the Internet, virtual meeting rooms, library repositories, and collaboration software all provide potential pathways to the experts.

As Meyers and her team establish these technologically based communication routes, people from one Y are already requesting information on what the experts at another Y are doing. The ease of access diminishes resistance that might otherwise be felt if people had to pick up the telephone or make an appointment to talk to an expert. Meyers admitted, though, that the biggest challenge has been finding skilled facilitators who can melt people's remaining resistance to sharing knowledge. To that end, she and her team have created terminology that makes sharing expertise and asking for expert help less threatening. For example, instead of using the term *best practice*, they have substituted *worked-for-me practice*. In this way, they personalize the practice and give people permission to share expertise that is their own rather than the property of someone else (the company).

To overcome resistances, American Express has mapped the human architecture of influencers in the organization. This map communicates not only who the thought leaders are but also that management endorses contacting these individuals when issues arise that require their assistance.

Similarly, Melissa worked with Motorola to facilitate networking among the staff. One of the tools she used was to ask the four hundred people in her program to list two people they wanted to meet, one internally and one externally. She explained that she would facilitate introductions and help to establish relationships. The nearly universal feedback she received was that in the past people would not hold out much hope of meeting these two individuals, but with Melissa providing the pathways, they not only were eager to get started but also believed that they would establish highly productive relationships.

Organizations, therefore, should go beyond identifying experts to make sure that people have access to them. This can mean providing maps and facilitators to provide introductions.

Many times, though, the best approach to this problem is the second solution of supporting existing communities and networks as places where experts make their expertise available. The diversity of these communities and their free-ranging discussions often catalyze experts to share information and ideas as they respond to the intellectual challenge of the debate.

Just as significant, when these communities evolve into wisdom networks focusing on key business issues, the identified experts in a particular area naturally gravitate toward them. They are able to communicate their expertise in a purposeful way. Subject matter experts, especially those who are well versed in topics crucial to achieving business goals, are pressed for time. Their knowledge is so valuable that sometimes access is limited by their availability. As part of a wisdom network, however, they are using their time wisely. They are making their expertise available to those pursuing major business goals. Rather than spreading their expertise too thin as identified experts, they can target it at top-priority business initiatives.

UBS works hard to establish pathways toward subject matter experts so that their expertise is used in the service of important business goals. As a result, the company has found many ways to encourage experts to share what they know and to think outside the box.

One such effort was within the company's huge operations department where senior leaders identified sixteen knowledge brokers and asked them to help encourage and garner ideas from all functions within the department throughout the world. The ideas could be on any aspect of the company, not just operations, as long as they were focused on increasing efficiency and productivity or reducing costs.

UBS set up an intranet site for the company's operations employees throughout the world to submit ideas. The sixteen knowledge brokers screened and responded to the ideas, telling submitters either why they weren't going to act on their ideas or why they were moving the idea up through the pipeline. In this way, even the people whose ideas weren't accepted felt that their effort was taken seriously. The knowledge brokers also worked hard to see that the accepted ideas were implemented. Due to the attention and support provided by the senior leaders, some incredibly creative ideas emerged. These ideas ranged from the simplest suggestions, such as recommending that the thousands of printers around the world be automatically turned off during the hours when they weren't used to save millions in electricity charges, to the more complicated, such as ways to increase the sharing of best practices among different regions to help increase productivity. It was this environment that enabled the company to pilot test some other concepts as well, one of which was a thank-you program—a peer recognition process for acknowledging individuals who were exhibiting the company's desired competencies and behavior above and beyond the norm. UBS provided small gifts to those individuals nominated by their peers who were clearly excelling in these areas.

This initiative linked one group of experts (the knowledge brokers) to another group (the operations department's subject matter experts), providing a process for moving innovative ideas into good programs and policies. Once you've identified the experts, you're in a much better position to create the right mix of people to achieve your organization's business objectives.

Know Your Experts and Identify Their Traits

All subject matter experts are not alike. By recognizing the differences among experts and identifying the specific traits that make them different, companies can mix and match people and put them into highly productive groups. A wisdom network cannot exist if all its members have the same traits. In fact, the Achilles' heel of many communities is that all their experts lack facilitation skills. Imagine a gathering of stereotypical rocket scientists—brilliant but nerdy—who possess a rare understanding of how to make rockets fly but are graceless, inarticulate, and paranoid. Their community would probably feature interesting discussions but lack an ability to achieve consensus on any one idea, translate it into a realistic program, or communicate it to those outside the community in a compelling, intelligible way.

Therefore, organizations should strive to create an effective mix of subject matter experts. This isn't necessary or even appropriate in the early ad hoc stages of grassroots groups. Early on, companies need to allow these communities the freedom to form and thrive on their own. In this initial stage, members forge relationships and build trust, necessary steps if the network is to grow and take on more challenging issues. Later, though, as communities grow and focus on magnet business topics, organizational leadership may consider creating an appropriate mix of expert traits.

Although wisdom networks are tangential to the business structure, leaders need to be aware of their composition, especially as they play increasingly more important roles. To that end, they should view these networks as jigsaw puzzles, attempting to match disparate people to create an effective whole. Although it is important to mix people from different functions, cultures, and generations to create a diverse network, it's just as important to create a good mixture of expert traits. Specifically, each expert in a wisdom network should possess at least one of the following traits:

- A demonstrated ability to talk regularly with people in other functions, departments, divisions, and offices
- The contacts and skills necessary to champion the network's ideas to the corporate hierarchy
- A talent for synthesizing ideas, resolving conflicts, and moving the group toward consensus
- A mentoring touch—the talent to bring out the best in other people in a network
- A high degree of creativity—the ability to see things from different perspectives and unusual angles
- A collaborative mind-set and associated skills
- An ability to lead discussions, and to facilitate and negotiate through brainstorming sessions
- A willingness to admit failures, to assess lessons learned and be able to leave ego at the door when collaborating

These complementary traits help wisdom networks to become self-sustaining. Not only do they turn a wide variety of knowledge into wisdom through these traits, but they also help the network to move quickly and effectively toward realistic cutting-edge ideas. By identifying these traits, companies can be assured that a network won't get bogged down in brainstorming and never be able to develop a concrete suggestion. Also, the groups won't falter because of political in-fighting or be dominated by one individual. Companies can feel confident that the network will make a concerted effort to push its best ideas out of the network and up into the organizational structure.

Nurture Collaboration

Of all these traits, the most valuable and most misunderstood is probably collaboration. The very nature of a wisdom network demands that at least some members possess this ability. The ability to collaborate is a trait that most people believe they have, but what they really mean is that they can work adequately with a small team of homogeneous people some of the time. True collaboration requires a willingness to trust others and inspire trust, an ability to acknowledge when someone else's idea is more effective than your own, and the adaptability to work well with a wide variety of people in many different situations. Identifying subject matter experts with these traits and encouraging them to participate in informal and formal networks greatly facilitates their effectiveness.

At one large corporation, a network evolved out of a community of practice around the issue of talent. The company was losing too many of its talented people and having trouble recruiting talent in the way it once did. The community included subject matter experts from throughout the company, coming together because the recent talent drain was of great concern to all of them as well as to management. In fact, management had encouraged several of these subject matter experts to join the community because a previous task force, charged with finding solutions to talent problems, had become so bitterly divided about solutions that it dissolved without making any recommendations.

While certain tensions also arose around this topic in the new community—some in the group felt strongly that the company should place greater emphasis on developing its own talent while others thought there should be greater emphasis on recruiting stars—the collaborators in the community defused these tensions effectively. When discussions became deadlocked, they brought in outside experts to help answer questions. When questions were raised about an idea the majority backed, members made an effort to research and benchmark in order to answer the questions to the minority's satisfaction. More than this, they provided the group with a flexibility that enabled them to adapt to new information and ideas as they went along, preventing the network from digging in on any early positions. Ultimately, they recommended a strategy to build bench strength in the company that management embraced and put into action.

Why Identification Is Essential for Learning Organizations

Learning organizations identify their subject matter experts. They realize that a significant percentage of these individuals need to be in decision-making roles or accessible in a leadership capacity to a wider audience than is typical. The traditional route to organizational prominence is by climbing the corporate ladder, and the people who often succeed in this endeavor usually possess good political skills, demonstrate an ability to execute and produce results, and are quintessential leadership types— inspirational, motivational, and decisive. Subject matter experts, on the other hand, do not always possess these qualities, nor is there often a clear career path for them, making their ascension more difficult.

It is problematic not only for the individual but also for organizations that recognize knowledge as a competitive advantage. When subject matter experts are visible, well connected, accessible, and in influential roles, they are able to disseminate their knowledge more effectively than if they are tucked away in a functional corner. They are in a better position to help others learn, and they are motivated to share what they know because of their increased prominence and influence.

We're not suggesting that companies immediately promote every subject matter expert they find to top management roles. Some of these experts have no interest in management positions, and others may not be particularly adept at management. Rather, companies must find a way to help these experts communicate their learning to as many people as possible.

Communities of practice, grassroots groups, and other types of wisdom networks offer experts forums to teach what they know and to increase the learning capacity of the company. Encouraging identified experts to participate in these groups doesn't just increase the number of people who can learn from them, but helps to direct the learning toward key business issues. In addition, when three or five or ten of these subject experts get together, their discussions create additional stores of knowledge. These people know so much about so many different things that when they talk, new concepts, conclusions, projects, and discoveries are inevitable.

This learning will not take place, however, if only a handful of subject experts is identified. Companies need to make a concerted effort to spotlight as many of them as possible, especially those whose knowledge is directly linked to strategic goals.

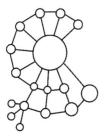

CHAPTER 8

Step 6: Create Organizational Stars— Acknowledge Wisdom

Traditionally, organizational stars rise through the hierarchy. By excelling in their areas of functional expertise, they gain great power and influence. Although they may be promoted into a leadership position and become responsible for multidisciplinary areas, their stardom usually relates to their functional abilities. Within a typical organization, sales stars, tech stars, manufacturing stars, and other specialized types are common. These people possess tremendous knowledge about how to get things done effectively, and they often produce outstanding results. These stars, however, rarely cross boundaries. Not only do they shine primarily within their functions but they have little interaction with people in other areas. In fact, the star software pro may not even be known to those outside of the MIS department.

Organizations that want to extract as much wisdom as possible from their employees must broaden the definition of what it means to be a star. Rather than limit the definition functionally, they should expand it to include individuals who shine within communities and networks, and who share their knowledge across functional and hierarchical boundaries. Unlike traditional stars who excel within the confines of their job description, these new stars transcend these descriptions. They provide information and ideas that benefit other functions besides their own and that address cutting-edge business topics that affect the entire organization.

Charles Dornbush, the founder, president, and CEO of Athenium, stated, "There is a real difference between management and leadership." Dornbush referred to the former category as the knowledge owners working to achieve their own targets and goals within their own functions or departments and the latter category as those who inspire others to engage in making changes happen and who lead the organization through boundary-crossing change. Although stars can be either managers or leaders, people who shine in wisdom networks come from the second group, and companies need to present these stars with opportunities to lead change efforts.

By creating awareness that the definition of stardom has been broadened, and highlighting the pathway to leadership through stardom in wisdom networks, companies motivate their experts to join and remain in wisdom networks. They communicate that there is more than one way to the top, and that the route may take them sideways.

How to Expand the Star System

In most companies, the mind-set of traditional stars is narrow and focused on achievement within a function or department. This is fine. You need these stars to get things done effectively. At the same time, if a company is lacking the new type of star, they are missing the people who can greatly facilitate organizational innovation. Because traditional stars tend to be most comfortable communicating with people in their functions and talking about functional issues, they usually don't engage in discussions with people who have very different backgrounds, skills, and ideas. They never push themselves to consider problems beyond their particular areas.

Therefore, it's no surprise that their ideas never rub up against a different set of ideas to create something that is cutting edge or even visionary. Although traditional stars may be innovative, they receive few if any opportunities to interact consistently with stars from other areas. As a result, they don't have the chance to experience the dynamic, boundary-crossing interactions that expand a person's creative range.

That is where the new network stars can shine. When companies not only support but reward these new stars with recognition, they encourage people to join networks, share their knowledge, and put organizational wisdom to more innovative use.

Although these two types of stars are different, they should not be separate. They need to work together to achieve organizational goals, and this means that they must appreciate each other's contributions. This tends to be a challenge for traditional stars. In many instances, they don't see how a wisdom network star based in another function will help them; they also don't see how a network star in their own function, who works cross-functionally in a network, will help them. Therefore, it is crucial that the company's leadership communicate that everyone wins in this two-star system. More specifically, leadership needs to convince traditional stars that these network stars will help them do their jobs even better than in the past.

Perhaps the best way to do this convincingly is by making sure wisdom networks and other top-level communities focus on magnet business topics. Traditional stars may view people in communities as dilettantes if they are working on nonessential topics. They see these people as hobbyists, concentrating on areas they love but that aren't of primary concern to the organization. When networks are targeting key business issues, however, their efforts will seem significant to traditional stars. In fact, we have found that when traditional stars are heads of departments or occupy any type of leadership position, they often want one of their people on these networks so they are kept aware of what is going on and how it might affect their functional efforts.

This two-tiered star system doesn't develop overnight. The emergence of network stars begins in grassroots groups where people may not be working on key business topics. Still, certain people shine in these groups, demonstrating a strong commitment to the group's goals, a tremendous amount of expertise, and consistent participation. At this point, they simply need encouragement from leaders in the company, especially the traditional stars. With this encouragement, they usually find their way to ad hoc groups addressing more important business topics, gaining skill at networking across boundaries, and working this parallel system to gather resources for and attention to their efforts.

At a certain point, their experience as networkers combined with their expertise will allow them to join a higher-level network, and within that network, they will emerge as a star. Over time, they will join other wisdom networks, shining in communities rather than within the command-and-control structure.

No hard and fast lines should separate traditional stars from network stars. Cross-pollination is welcome, and it may be that a traditional star joins a network because he or she is passionate about and expert in a given topic and wants to explore it in a nontraditional manner. It may also be that a network star is chosen for a task force or team created by management because either this person's expertise on a key business topic is crucial for the company's future success or the organization is flattening out and needs more network stars in leadership roles.

The Benefits: Why a Two-Star System Adds Value

Some might argue that any type of star is a negative rather than a positive in organizational life. Their premise would be that in team-intensive structures where work is done through collaboration and consensus, individual stars are an anachronism. The anti–star system perspective would assert that deifying individual accomplishment is counterproductive because teams should be the stars rather than individuals.

Despite the popularity of team-based structures in certain industries, hierarchy is alive and well in most companies of any size, the exception being smaller entrepreneurial and high-tech companies where innovation is often their driving force. In fact, what we're finding is that large organizations tend to be of two minds when it comes to their organizational structure. They want the best of both worlds—the execution that comes from a command-and-control model and the innovation that comes from a flattened one.

Given the coexistence of these two structures, it makes sense that two types of stars are necessary to satisfy the requirements of both. Although some stars can be prima donnas and work more for themselves than their groups or organizations, most are able to satisfy their own egos and organizational performance standards quite nicely. Network stars, especially, often have a strong communal mentality because they understand the value of working through diverse collaborations and relish the opportunity. This doesn't mean they lack an ego, only that they know how to manage it. We should also point out that large corporations, especially, have a rich history of star performers whose innovative ideas and ability to get things done have driven their organizations to great accomplishments. Therefore, we're convinced that the star system is positive, and that the two-tiered star system is doubly positive. In particular, the two-tiered system accomplishes the following:

1. Facilitates execution and innovation

Companies usually are top-heavy with stars who, as we've seen, operate on a particular set of assumptions that mitigates against sharing certain types of knowledge. At the same time, they assume that they must know their area of responsibility backwards and forwards and use that knowledge in the most efficient way possible. This makes strong execution possible.

Another important group, we call them *anticipators,* is often in short supply, especially in starring roles. These individuals look forward to sharing their knowledge with great anticipation. They are excited about forums that allow them to exchange information and ideas with others. They especially anticipate interactions where idea exchanges occur with a diverse group of people. Rather than feel threatened by such exchanges, they embrace them. They relish the chance to hear fresh and sometimes radical perspectives, and they also enjoy proposing ideas that may threaten the status quo. Although these people may not be as good at executing as the functional stars, they are much better at innovation.

A two-tiered star system, therefore, creates a good balance between people with execution skills and those who are proficient at innovating.

2. Improves recruitment and retention

Talent management has become a topic of great concern in most corporations, and a two-tiered star system is an excellent talent management tool.

Although some people are attracted to the traditional command-and-control hierarchy, others are not. Some highly talented people are not looking for vertical ladders to success but alternative, horizontal options. Organizations that can offer stardom through wisdom networks attract people who are naturals at idea generation and exchange. These networkers want to join companies where they can be successful even if they are not command-and-control types. They are searching for opportunities to advance through their knowledge rather than through their ability to delegate or make decisions. Wisdom networks provide career paths that traverse silos. They also are laboratories for people to practice new skills and to test their cutting-edge ideas without having to jeopardize execution by practicing and testing on the job.

Just as significantly, many highly knowledgeable people reflexively look outside the company for opportunities when they become bored with their jobs or feel they've stopped learning. A second type of star system offers them internal opportunities, chances to break out of their roles via participation in ad hoc groups.

Traditional stars often do what they do because they enjoy the power and the perks that come with stardom. Network stars may enjoy fame and fortune, too, but they also do what they do because they love to learn new things and express what they've learned. When companies make it clear that they support network stars, they give a percentage of their experts a raison d'être. Although they must still perform in their functional roles, they have the chance to explore other roles and to interact with a wide range of other experts who have a good deal to teach them. For them, the thrill of work is research and brainstorming, pushing the edge of the envelope in search of new ways of doing things. Discovery turns them on, and in a two-tiered star system, numerous forums exist for discovery.

As a result, they don't feel compelled to look elsewhere for more intellectually stimulating work. Nor do they have to feel guilty or as if they are wasting their time (from a career standpoint) by participating in communities. When companies recognize the importance of these idea exchanges by conferring star status on networkers, they communicate that participation in communities is anything but a waste of time.

3. Builds the reservoir of organizational wisdom

Network stars create organizational knowledge at an exponential rate. Every node (person) added to the network creates a potential increase in wisdom, and if these nodes are stars, it's even more likely that wisdom will increase. So much of the expertise in a company is isolated in corporate corners. In any segment of any department, an expert usually exists, but this person rarely gets a chance to spread his or her knowledge beyond the limits of his or her team or function. When companies make it clear that an alternative path to stardom exists through ad hoc, knowledge-sharing groups, these experts are motivated to emerge from their functional corners.

When these experts have the chance to talk with experts from other areas of the company, they often come up with new ideas and insights, some of which have immediate, practical value for the company while some have long-term value. When these provocative ideas start circulating through a company's networks, they stimulate more thinking from other experts, and additional wisdom is created.

Stardom is a powerful incentive for joining, staying in, and making the most out of knowledge-sharing outlets. It seems like such a simple thing when we write about it, but in reality, it requires a significant amount of time and effort. Experts by definition are in great demand and under stress to produce great results. The last thing they need is one more demand on their time. The chance for stardom, though, is a powerful motivator, as is the opportunity to learn and tackle challenging new projects.

Why a Star Might Choose a Network Career Path

Some organizations worry that endorsing a network star career path might prove futile. They doubt that someone might choose to shine in a wisdom network rather than in the traditional command-and-control structure.

This worry is understandable, but it is also groundless. Certainly, some people prefer the rewards of being a traditional star. They relish the power that comes with the territory. They enjoy operating strictly within a function or at a certain hierarchical level. Other people, though, want a different type of work life or at least a supplemental experience to their functional jobs. What drives them is learning. For them, the traditional star path becomes boring after a certain point. They find little reward in solving the same problems in the same way day after day.

This alternative star path also offers an alternative route up the corporate ladder. Typically, stars are promoted into higher-level managerial positions. This is a reward, but at the same time, it punishes them for, and deprives their organizations of, their subject matter expertise. In managerial roles, these stars have less opportunity to apply their expertise to problems and opportunities. Instead, they spend increasing amounts of time on department management, human resources, legal, and other administrative issues. What many experts really want is to spend as much time as possible using their expertise in new and important ways. More than if they remained in traditional roles, being a network star makes it possible for people to engage in learning and exchanging ideas and still work on challenging projects, applying their particular expertise.

We should also point out that in every organization there are experts whose knowledge is underutilized. Most of their time is spent putting out little fires instead of big ones or focusing on routine, parochial projects rather than on ones that have organization-wide impact. They are acutely aware that they have more to offer the company than they are providing. They have ideas about how the company can change a process or policy, but they feel constrained by their title or role and remain silent.

Tim, for instance, was a marketing executive in the beverage division of a major food company. His organization had a number of failed new product introductions, especially in the frozen-food area, and Tim was itching to suggest a new product concept. In fact, he spent many nights and weekends researching the market, creating the product from scratch, and tinkering with it until he had the ingredients right, figuring out various cost-and-profit scenarios and creating a product introduction strategy.

To do this work, Tim crossed boundaries he never could have crossed in his regular job, where his work was confined to beverages. He had been told on more than one occasion to leave the research to the R&D people. Tim, though, was a genius at new product introductions. He had a fierce drive to take on new assignments where he could put his genius to use in different ways. When Tim approached the head of the marketing department about his idea for a frozen-food product, he was rebuffed. The marketing head thanked him for his effort, but he admitted that he would have to endure so much flak from other division and department heads if he moved Tim's idea into the project stage that it wouldn't be worth it.

A few communities existed in Tim's company, and he joined one that was focused on new products. However, he found that although the other community members were enthusiastic, many of them were not experts. He also knew these communities were a sop thrown to employees and that no idea to emerge from them would ever amount to anything. Truth be told, the culture was not particularly amenable to knowledge sharing.

Tim eventually resigned and found a job at an organization with a more enlightened attitude toward communities and networks. Tim had star potential, but he couldn't realize it with his former employer.

What Organizations Should Do to Create Additional Star Power

To create a network star system, companies don't have to go to the effort and expense of setting up a horizontal work track and enlisting the HR department to create specs around this network path. Instead, they need to take simpler steps to communicate that it is possible and desirable for people to achieve star status through their performance and leadership in ad hoc groups as well as through more formalized departments and teams.

Specifically, here are the steps we recommend:

1. Spread the word that network participation helps people to do their jobs better

Company leaders must disabuse their staff of the notion that participation in groups is a sacrifice that will make their lives more difficult. They can do this by communicating how membership in a network provides insights and ideas that increase job effectiveness. They need to use formal and informal tools—corporate memos, online bulletins, e-mail notices, as well as casual conversation—to demonstrate that sacrifice is not an appropriate description for what participating in a network requires.

In the mid-1990s, Buckman Labs brilliantly linked participation in knowledge exchanges with job performance. As a company specializing in chemicals with a large, global sales force, Buckman Labs recognized that its greatest asset was knowledge rather than chemicals. Bob Buckman, the CEO, was a true knowledge visionary who put the entire sales force online, with supporting communities of knowledge specialists available at their fingertips through IBM Thinkpads. During client presentations, salespeople who didn't know the answer to a question queried the Buckman knowledge network and received an instant response. Clients were impressed, and so too were the salespeople, who saw that knowledge increased their client service capabilities and helped make sales. Bob Buckman preached the gospel of connectivity, and he did so consistently and passionately to the point that every one of his one thousand–plus employees got the message. Salespeople stopped thinking of their Thinkpads as accessories and started believing they were necessities. Time after time, a salesperson would come back from a presentation and talk about how the knowledge it accessed instantly helped clinch the deal.

Stories like these will quickly circulate throughout a company and make everyone aware that participation in a network can help produce star-like results. As soon as people realize that networking is actually a valuable resource to help them to perform their jobs, the take-up is incredibly fast. This will even motivate a traditional star to participate in a network or to encourage one of his or her own experts to participate. In either case, these stories legitimize networks.

2. Give network leaders the star treatment

In most companies, traditional stars receive perks and privileges that other employees don't, and these informal benefits let everyone know that these individuals are special. When a tech star requests time off to attend a conference halfway around the world—and asks if his or her two top people can come along—this request is usually granted. If a star says something is important, management takes this person at his or her word. When a sales star recommends that a satellite office be set up in a customer's headquarters to facilitate service, the company usually rubber-stamps this recommendation.

Network stars should receive the same respect. Their requests for resources should be honored. They should be granted the freedom to balance their day jobs and their network responsibilities as they see fit. In short, they should be treated in a way that everyone in the company knows that they are stars, even if their stardom is confined to wisdom networks.

3. Run programs that encourage interaction between traditional and network stars

For the two-tiered star system to work, both groups of stars must respect and support one another. When traditional stars resent or are dismissive of their network brethren, they may sabotage the efforts of the networkers. For instance, Jack is a star sales executive who resents that one of his star salespeople, Jennifer, is a member of a community that is addressing bureaucratic issues. Her group is looking at ways of streamlining processes and policies by cutting red tape in order to get things done with the greatest speed possible. Jack has been grumbling about the time that Jennifer and others devote to this community work, and when the community comes up with three recommendations that are bumped up to the company's executive committee, Jack convinces the committee not to act on any of the recommendations. Furthermore, he discourages Jennifer from participating in this or any other ad hoc group and tells her to devote her time to rising up the sales ranks as he did.

Traditional stars who fight recommendations that come out of networks and who discourage experts from participating in them diminish the wisdom available to organizations. Many times, this problem can be solved by setting up programs that facilitate interactions between traditional and emerging network stars. UBS created a pilot program that paired highly successful, experienced branch managers (traditional stars) with younger, rising stars—also branch managers—creating a wisdom network of diverse skill and experience levels. The idea was that the older managers would share their experience with the younger stars, and the younger stars would suggest innovative approaches of which the older ones might not be aware. At the end of the year, both "partners" would receive a performance review that would take the combined performance of both their branches into account.

It was a successful pilot test, but not because branch performances were consistently and measurably better or worse because of the pairing. The best result of the program was that all the participants said that even if UBS decided not to roll out the program, they wanted to continue working with their partners in the following year.

This type of program increases the odds that stars on different career paths will support each other even though one is moving vertically and the other is traveling horizontally.

4. Monitor what topics the stars are addressing in their various ad hoc groups

If your organization has many thriving communities and networks, no doubt some of them will focus on topics that are tangential to or largely unrelated to major business issues. That's fine, since it is not the organization's job to dictate topics to every ad hoc group under its roof. Management should be cognizant, however, that if the company's true experts are spending their time in networks that are addressing tangential issues, the programs will be open to criticism that they are simply a hobby. This provides ammunition for critics who may view communities and networks as frivolous activities unrelated to the company's core purpose.

Stars who join networks should be encouraged to focus their groups on key business topics. This may mean that people in leadership positions should talk to these network stars and suggest they join a specific network that is addressing a key issue. Management may also need to do a better job communicating what the business's magnet topics are so that groups form around them.

In most instances, experts naturally gravitate toward these topics. At times, though, they become enmeshed in the esoterica of their specialized areas and lose sight of the bigger picture. To avoid this scenario, organizations should be aware of what network stars are spending their time on.

5. Track and support the evolution of network stars

The traditional path to stardom within the corporate hierarchy is clearly marked. First, individuals must acquire certain skills and knowledge.

Then, they must achieve a certain level of results. Next, they must exceed this level on a consistent basis. Over a period of time, they are recognized as the experts and become the go-to people when challenging problems or great opportunities emerge. They are rewarded for their expertise through financial compensation, promotions, and other perks.

The evolution of a network star is less clearly delineated. In fact, these stars are often invisible as they become highly proficient at skills such as crossing boundaries, securing resources to further network goals, gaining management support for network ideas, and so on. They are off the company radar. No one from human resources measures their progress and notes their evolving skills. No one steers them into training programs or has them attend development workshops. Their evolution toward star status is essentially left to chance.

If management pays little or no attention to the opportunity of developing this career path, these budding network stars can easily become discouraged and reduce or drop their involvement in communities, perhaps even in the development of their subject matter expertise. If they are not given support along the way, they may feel the company doesn't value their participation and skills outside of their immediate job function.

Although it's important that management avoid trying to control communities, management can take a few small actions to encourage the evolution of stars and, as a consequence, the impact of the communities. Specifically, management should:

- Be aware of the most active participants in various communities and those who are separating themselves from the pack through their leadership and ideas.

- Offer verbal recognition and encouragement to the people who seem to be emerging as stars.

- Provide them with resources as they evolve into stars—coaching, mentoring, contacts with outside experts, opportunities to put their ideas to use on projects and programs—so that their development within a wisdom network is accelerated.

The Synergy of Wisdom and Execution

Organizations that have an excess of execution and not enough wisdom will fail as innovators. Organizations that have a great deal of wisdom and little execution ability will fail in implementation of ideas, or execution. The key, therefore, is finding the proper balance between the two.

When both traditional and network stars are accessible through a wisdom network medium, a continuous source of proven experience and fresh thinking is available on every key issue. When companies are faced with a crisis or an opportunity, this wisdom gives them options. Often, time is critical and the availability of tapping into the expertise of wisdom networks on the spur of the moment can mean the difference between landing a million-dollar deal and second place. The stars have freedom to suggest options outside of the routine way and can tailor their approach to fit the situation, while a network will invariably provide an alternative to the norm that might be a much more effective and pertinent solution.

At the same time, the company isn't awash in ideas and lacking the ability to choose the right one. It can create a plan and execute it quickly, qualitatively, and cost-effectively. In most instances, implementation combined with innovation yields superior results.

At UBS and other companies with strong knowledge-sharing networks in place, two types of stars not only coexist but support one another's efforts. In each organization, management has made a concerted effort to throw its support behind network stars, making sure everyone recognizes that they are not a flavor of the month but as much a part of the culture as vanilla and chocolate. Although supporting efforts vary from company to company, they usually employ the following three methods:

1. *Put accolades in writing.* In other words, management provides "official" recognition that network leaders are accomplishing significant goals and are due respect. A printed recognition carries weight, whether it is printed in a memo or the company newsletter.

2. *Use ceremonies to celebrate success.* Dinners, parties, awards functions, and other forums serve notice that network stars are being honored. Every organization has its celebratory rituals, and when network leaders are integrated into these rituals, they gain stature in the organization.

3. *Endorse new ideas.* This is the most significant acknowledgment that network leaders enjoy star status. When leadership embraces ideas that bubble up from ad hoc groups and turns them into programs and policies, employees quickly grasp that network leaders are making significant contributions.

Obviously, these three actions need to be taken consistently and over time, but eventually, everyone in an organization will grasp that new stars are rising.

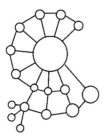

CHAPTER 9

Step 7: Ideas Are Not Enough—Provide Implementation Options

Critics of communities and other ad hoc groups often complain that nothing comes out of these groups but ideas. They believe that communities are nothing more than think tanks, spinning out one creative but unusable idea after another. At worst, these critics believe that they are a complete waste of time.

It is understandable how an outsider might develop this perspective. If you either have never been a member of one of these ad hoc groups or were a member of one that spun its wheels trying to spin out ideas, you may believe that they have no practical value for the organization. This attitude, if it becomes widespread, can become a self-fulfilling prophecy.

No doubt, some communities do spend their time working on marginal (to the business) topics or coming up with highly imaginative new programs and projects that are absolutely unfeasible. When this happens too often, it gives knowledge management and related activities a bad name, since a steady diet of off-the-wall, unusable ideas will turn anyone off.

159

In a true wisdom network, however, implementation options are always being considered. As intellectually stimulating as members might find discussions with fellow experts, they are driven to turn ideas into reality, plans into projects, and thought into action. They seek to deliver new products and services that benefit the company or to streamline processes that can drastically reduce inefficiencies and cut costs. When a wisdom network hits on an idea that excites everyone, the next step is always to figure out the best way to test and use it.

Four Ways to Turn Talk into Action

Wisdom networks don't need to reinvent the wheel. They don't need to build new pathways to move their ideas out of the discussion stage into projects and programs. To do so would engender turf battles, require a new budget item, and create many other problems. It also would violate the spirit of wisdom networks, which involves capitalizing on the system that exists rather than inventing an entirely new system. Wisdom networks understand that these same internal processes are an extremely valuable resource to them, to help them move an idea out of the network and turn it into a project or pilot test. In this way, wisdom networks actually reinforce the existing structure, offering teams and functions fresh opportunities to shine. When a new idea's implementation requirements stretch the capabilities of the company, they must have options for putting their ideas into practice. Here are four common options to which every network should have access:

1. Create a new project team

A wisdom network can identify the people who are best able to make the group's idea happen. These people can find a sponsor to provide support and credibility for the network and a budget holder to fund the efforts and oversee the deliverables needed to make it real. All this may sound pedestrian, but it often requires that a network accept that an existing department may be in the best position to implement the network's concept.

When a recommendation emerges from a staff member, community, or network, management—especially true in organizations that don't have much of a history of knowledge sharing—may be reluctant to approve resources for a project team to take this idea to the next stage. What facilitates approval is a powerful network champion and an idea aimed at a magnet business topic. In most instances, need overcomes tradition. If an idea could potentially solve a critical business problem that the company has heretofore been unable to solve, green lights are usually given to project teams.

2. Latch on to an existing similar project or program

When it seems unlikely that a project team will receive approval or when requests are turned down, this is a viable option. When networks are working on key business topics, it's likely that other groups within the organization are focused on these same issues.

Although structured teams are probably taking a more traditional approach and may be more functionally homogeneous, they may feel stymied or need fresh thinking. Often, structured teams become frustrated because their in-the-box ideas don't help them meet ambitious goals, and they are overjoyed when they find out-of-the-box ideas that do meet those goals.

Network members can approach these traditional teams to see whether they would be interested in the network's ideas. We have found that if the head of an existing project or program values innovative thinking, he or she generally will be receptive to the network-created idea and may even ask some members of the network to participate on the existing team.

3. Launch a short-lived task force

This is a pre-implementation step, but one that may greatly increase the odds that a wisdom network's idea is executed successfully. If the network has come up with an idea that is sweeping in nature and requires significant organizational change, a task force makes sense. The bigger the change, the greater is the need to assess the implications for different functions and departments.

A task force is composed of experts from many different areas within the company and can brainstorm the change implications, recommending the best way to test or roll out the idea into programs, and subsequently support the execution of change. In this way, a network increases the odds that its idea won't be dismissed as unrealistic or overly ambitious. The task force can deal with any political issues by ensuring that each political element is represented on the task force, as well as including on the task force department representatives who will be involved in implementation. For instance, one wisdom network came up with an innovative plan for global growth, which is a top priority for the organization. The plan was very different from the one that the company had been pursuing (and pursuing without much success). As part of the plan, the network recommended consolidating certain European offices as well as opening new offices in emerging markets. Network members knew that their plan would send shock waves through the organization unless introduced and implemented with great care, so they worked with their sponsor to form a task force that ultimately recommended breaking the plan into stages and creating an implementation team for each stage. The task force was composed of staff from every department, office, and location involved in the change, giving responsibility to the people whom the change would impact the most.

4. Take the idea back to where you came from

Someone in the network may be in the perfect position to bring the idea back to his or her team or function and let them pilot test it or move it forward in some other way. Sometimes, the timing is perfect and the network member is in a good position to use his or her day job to implement a concept. For instance, Linda is a manufacturing executive who is a member of a network focusing on creating user-friendly technological systems. For years, the product development department has had the company's most complex and user-unfriendly systems, and people have complained bitterly about them. Linda became very frustrated having to deal with complaints about the system every day, while also attempting to ensure her team met its performance quota. She reached out to her peers in different product lines, and began to discuss with them the inefficiencies of the technologies used by each team. Linda found that each of her peers' teams were similarly hampered, often struggling to overcome what each thought should have been easy tasks. Linda's network came up with a model for a new system that would work company-wide, volunteering her department to immediately test the model, knowing that if it merely decreased employee complaints the benefit in employee job satisfaction would be great enough to help increase productivity. Given the leadership Linda provided, and her commitment to use her team to test implementation options, other teams jumped on board immediately.

This option, obviously, shouldn't be used if there is an uncomfortable fit between the idea and the network member's department. The last thing the network wants is the perception that it's shoving an idea down a reluctant department head's throat. Our point is that wisdom network members have the option to take new concepts back to their "home" team.

Overcoming Resistance to Implementation Options

As we've suggested, resistance to implementation is minimal when a network is filled with the right experts working on the right business topics, and when the network has a champion who promotes his or her cause to management and when sponsors provide solid support. Unfortunately, not every ad hoc group is working in these ideal circumstances, making it difficult for the group to become a true wisdom network.

Most communities have a good sense of how much resistance they're likely to encounter when they try to implement an idea, based on their knowledge of the culture and the track record of ad hoc groups turning ideas into projects and pilot tests. They also are aware of which ideas are likely to meet the most resistance, because any concept that challenges the status quo is going to be tough for a network to sell.

Although great ideas can sell themselves, more often than not even the best ideas need help. We know more than one community that was so excited by the idea that emerged from its discussions that members assumed everyone would be similarly excited and supportive. In reality, people can respond to great ideas that emerge from an informal group with suspicion and jealousy. Therefore, don't be naive about what it takes to reach the implementation stage.

People are sometimes stymied when it comes to these four options because they are naive about the implementation process or because they fail to realize that they even have these four different options available to them. As a result, they become frustrated and give up when one doesn't work. At other times, they aren't sufficiently strategic about how to melt resistance and gain implementation acceptance. Here are some things to consider that might help networks effectively overcome this resistance:

1. Internal road shows

Wisdom networks possess at least one individual to champion their cause, someone with organizational clout and the ability to speak persuasively on behalf of the network's concept. One method of espousing the network's cause is to provide "road shows"—conferences, speaking engagements, and other communication forums—where the champion delivers messages that the network wants the organization to hear. Sometimes, these road shows must be targeted at one person, such as the executive who can authorize a project team. In other instances, such as when a task force must be created because the idea requires systemic change, everyone from budget heads to various committees must be lobbied.

The purpose of these road shows is twofold: (1) to communicate the value of the idea and (2) to validate the wisdom network that created it. This last goal is significant because people may discount a great idea because of its source. It is possible, however, that an idea may encounter a great deal of resistance despite a champion's best efforts. This may be a sign that there is something wrong with the idea itself or that larger political or business issues are creating roadblocks. In these instances, the wisdom network should reconvene to evaluate the reasons for the rejection and determine what needs to be changed to move the idea toward implementation—or if the network should go back to the drawing board.

2. The learning curve factor

Road shows should be part of a broader education process in which community and network participants continually educate their colleagues and bosses about how they offer a fresh source of innovation for the organization. Too often, companies fall into innovation ruts. They become accustomed to turning to specific individuals within the company when they need a new approach or a cutting-edge concept. They don't realize that the grassroots groups that have formed on their own—the communities of practice and interest and the wisdom networks—all have tremendous innovation potential. They don't understand that the diverse nature of these groups, their willingness to cross boundaries, and their high level of expertise all can tap into ideas that otherwise would remain hidden from the organizational view.

It takes time before a wide swath of management is aware of the value of these networks, and it is up to network participants to educate them. This isn't a one-time effort. It's not enough to mention to your boss once or twice what took place during a community meeting. Although different people will climb the learning curve at different rates, they won't climb it at all if they aren't made aware of all the exciting developments taking place in communities on a continuous basis. As the terms *community of interest, ad hoc group,* and *wisdom network* become part of the organizational vocabulary, these groups will begin to gain credibility in management's eyes. Once they gain credibility, it becomes much easier to obtain approval for a project team or other implementation options.

3. Selectivity in ideas chosen for implementation

Here are some common mistakes communities make when they try to move an idea into an implementation pathway:

• *A relatively young community recommends a relatively large change program.* Because the group has not established a good track record, its recommendation is viewed skeptically. The team members seem to be biting off more than they can chew, and they are viewed as unrealistic.

• *An ad hoc group bombards the company with implementation recommendations.* Too many ideas spoil the broth. It's terrific when a network comes up with a large number of innovative ideas, but the group members need to winnow the list down to the top ones. They can easily overwhelm people with one idea after the next, and management can question their motivation because it may seem that they are trying to impress others with their creativity rather than focusing on ideas that will really help the organization achieve key business goals.

• *A community recommends actions for ideas that aren't cost effective.* This is not to say that the group should avoid any proposals that are expensive; sometimes, big ideas require big budgets. If the reward doesn't seem worth the financial risk, the members' requests to move forward will be turned down.

When wisdom networks are in their formative stages, it often makes sense to start small and build on successive accomplishments. By targeting smaller but important problems and opportunities, networks can demonstrate that they know what they are doing while learning and becoming organizationally wiser. One project that is implemented successfully begets another one. In this way, networks build their credibility throughout the company and can get approval for increasingly larger projects or ones that vary from the norm, such as cultural change programs that are tough for staff to accept and implement.

4. The need for members to participate in implementation

We have found that some members of communities share the misconception that they are only idea-generators or thinkers. As a result, they make little or no effort to move an idea out of the discussion stage and capitalize on any of the available implementation options. Perhaps the most egregious mistake is not taking an idea back to their function when they are in the perfect position to do so. Although not all members of wisdom networks are in a position to implement ideas, they often can take advantage of at least one of the four options.

A Wisdom Network's Natural Implementation Resources

In any large organization, people constantly vie for limited resources, and they always complain about how their team's project was shot down for no apparent reason or for what seems like a bad reason. Many times, the reasons are sound. In other instances, large organizations simply don't have the processes in place to separate the wheat from the chaff at the project level.

Wisdom networks have three distinct advantages when it comes to implementation.

1. Wisdom networks have great connections throughout the company

Networking across functions and hierarchical levels is a wisdom networker's attribute, and it means that people in networks have a stronger circle of contacts that they can rely upon than others. People can usually tap into their personal networks to facilitate implementation. Unlike other teams, their contacts aren't limited to one function or one hierarchical level. If they need additional funding for a pilot test, they probably have a connection with someone who can facilitate that funding. If they need to find out who else is working on a similar issue so they might piggyback their idea onto an existing project, they have the contacts to discover a compatible project.

2. Wisdom networks are highly resilient

Wisdom networks are able to learn from their failures and do better each time they attempt to implement a new innovative concept. Therefore, when their recommendations are turned down, they treat the rejection as a challenge. Rather than becoming discouraged and giving up, they discuss why the idea was rejected, whether the reasons were valid, and what—if anything—can be done to revive interest in implementation. Wisdom networks are learning laboratories, and they recognize that failure is a rich source of knowledge. Rather than giving up in frustration, they assess the situation with an eye toward other options. In their analysis of what went wrong, they ask the following questions:

- Was there something inherently wrong with the idea; did it deserve to be rejected?
- If we were to reconceive the idea based on the reason for rejection, might it have a better chance of being implemented; do we believe the idea would be as good in its reconceived state or would it be watered down and not worth implementing?
- Might we stand a better chance of implementing the idea if we pursued one of the three remaining implementation options (as opposed to the one that was used and didn't work)? If so, which of the three options would work best?

You may recall our discussion of the UBS wisdom network that attempted to help the organization capitalize on grid technology. In the beginning, the network hoped to achieve economies of scale by sharing infrastructure components across different teams and departments. In the past, these teams and departments purchased their own hardware and servers and ran their own databases, a highly inefficient and costly approach. Grid computing, theoretically, could remedy this problem.

The UBS network, after much brainstorming, came up with a plan that allowed all these different groups to share hardware components by using grid software, but as the plan moved toward implementation, it met with great resistance. The departments were too dissimilar from one another for a common interface to work. Each department had long traditions of operating independently, building its own solutions tailored to its specific group of business users, with each solution designed exclusively to work with all the systems and processes of the particular department's function. Attempting to come up with standard solutions across these silo business departments had been attempted in the past with very little success.

This wisdom network asked itself some questions like the ones previously mentioned, and recognized that its grid computing concept was still viable, but that the network needed a narrower, more focused target if it would ever have a chance of working across these departments. After a great deal of research and discussion, the network hit on a hybrid approach in which different groups use certain proprietary systems in some areas but use grid technology where clear commonalities exist. The hybrid approach allowed each team the ability to keep its uniquely tailored solutions while supporting the development of underlying synergies that saved each of them money.

3. Wisdom networks are tuned in to the new way of getting things done

In the past, execution in organizations was largely accomplished through position power. Although hierarchical power is still necessary for execution, collaboration and influence are increasingly important. Too often, the typical organizational team is task oriented and linear. Team members adhere to schedules and methodologies, and they follow the instructions of the team leader. They tend to collaborate in name only, because they don't display the openness, flexibility, and willingness to cross boundaries that marks true collaborative efforts.

Wisdom networks are filled with people who collaborate on a higher level. They are completely forthcoming about their ideas and information, eager to engage in debate and discussion. Because networks aren't part of the structured system, participants don't have to collaborate "on demand." They can take their time and don't feel compelled to drive toward consensus or make decisions about what to do because they have a deadline to meet. They are also more driven by the idea itself rather than individual glory, because they relish the chance to use their expertise in the best way possible. The people in wisdom networks are passionate experts, and as such, they persuade and motivate through the sheer force of their expertise and near-spiritual commitment. When they say to their functional boss or a top executive, "This is a terrific idea that should be implemented," their words carry a lot of weight. They can obtain resources and garner support through their inspiration and expertise that might not be available to other teams.

Assess Your Group's Implementation Capabilities

A wisdom network of impassioned experts that has established a track record for coming up with highly effective programs and projects will have a much easier time implementing its ideas than an ad hoc group or community with few (if any) experts that has minimal excitement around the subject or no history of effective idea generation. This is especially true if the network is part of an organization that is driven to find the most innovative ideas no matter what their source.

Therefore, you can determine a given group's capacity to implement based on the following paired questions:

1A. Are most people in a community or network experts who exhibit true passion for their expertise; are they known in their particular work teams or functions as "go-to" people; are they truly energized and committed to their work, using their knowledge to be cutting edge and innovative?

1B. Are the people in a community or network knowledgeable but not necessarily the experts in their areas; are they interested in the topic under discussion but relatively unenthusiastic or unwilling to expend the time and effort to push the envelope, preferring to maintain the status quo?

2A. Is your organization one where various communities and networks have been in existence for years; is the culture such that experts receive explicit and implicit encouragement to join ad hoc groups and pursue hot business topics; is your company's management a strong supporter of knowledge sharing in general and wisdom networks specifically?

2B. Is your company relatively new to the concept of knowledge sharing; are the communities that exist generally viewed as hobbies and not taken seriously; is it rare for an idea that emerged from a community to become an actual project or program that helped change the company?

3A. Is your company committed to innovation to the point that the source of ideas is unimportant; is management quick to spot a truly creative concept and find a way to support it, even if it has emerged from outside the traditional system; do people in communities feel free to float untraditional or boundary-crossing approaches without fear of stepping on someone's toes?

3B. Does your organization suffer from a not-invented-here complex; do even strong, fresh ideas get rejected because they were suggested by a person or group from another function or without the proper credentials; does the company rely on a relatively small number of people for creative ideas?

Clearly, if you answered the first questions in each pair affirmatively, you probably have more implementation options and an easier time exercising them. However, this doesn't mean that the only good community or network is one with strong implementation capabilities. Realistically, it takes time before communities of interest evolve into wisdom networks that can not only come up with new innovations but also find the means to implement them.

At first, communities may need to experience growing pains before they attract passionate experts and gain widespread management support. Even companies with mature wisdom networks, however, should still have a flourishing system of grassroots and ad hoc groups. To put it in baseball terms, these ad hoc groups are the company's farm system, providing valuable experience in brainstorming, benchmarking, and boundary crossing. They also help individuals find their proper roles within this alternative universe. Some people are better suited to be facilitators while others are champions in training.

Ideas are the lifeblood of every company, and they should be treated with great respect. Learning organizations value idea generation, and they try to create an environment in which numerous forums exist for the exchange of information and ideas. Grassroots communities of interest may not have the capability of doing much with their ideas on their own, but they may be capable of coming up with original thinking and provocative approaches. Bubbling them up to a community with greater implementation capabilities is a viable option.

Finally, implementation is often a matter of situation and need. Sometimes, management simply wants to stimulate creative thinking on an emerging business topic. Management may not be ready to talk about executing an idea, wanting only to start the idea machine. It may also have a specific business objective that precludes implementation.

An organization, for instance, may want to find ways to increase a key competency—for example, development of direct reports to ensure leadership and skill continuity. This is a critical need for any company, and although the organization may have set formal teams to work on this goal, the company could easily be dissatisfied with the result. Therefore, a community or network that is good at getting things done will need to identify best practices for succession planning, and try to develop specific recommendations on how the company can help its managers acquire this skill. Given management support and a clear business need, this network will likely have all four implementation options at its disposal.

Learn the Secret: How Things Really Get Done

Every company has both formal and informal ways of getting things done. The former consists of clearly delineated lines of command and protocols for moving projects forward. Steps in this formal process demand that paperwork be completed, budgets allocated, and so on. In essence, this is the slow, bureaucratic, orderly way of executing, and for many objectives, it is the best system.

Things can also be accomplished informally. Red tape can be cut, budgets can be tweaked to get money when it seemed that none was available, and support for a pilot test can be secured even when it seemed the project was dead in the water. A relatively small number of experts in a company possess the shrewdness to get things done in this informal manner. Generally, they are the grizzled veterans who have been through the wars or the aggressive newcomers who have yet to recognize their limits. Each knows how and when to do end runs around the system to fix problems or to accelerate work to meet tight deadlines, although the grizzled veteran will make fewer mistakes. Not every expert in a company possesses this ability—some have great knowledge and skills but not much savvy. The experts we're referring to are adaptive and imaginative, and their motto is, "If it can be done, I will find a way to do it."

An infinite number of ways exist to take advantage of the talents of these implementing experts, and we certainly don't want to imply that the ways suggested here are the only ones. BP Amoco, for instance, divides its communities into *enabling* and *delivery* networks. The former are similar to communities of practice, in that knowledgeable employees exchange job-related expertise and discuss what methods work best. Delivery networks, on the other hand, are knowledge communities with clear-cut business goals. As their name implies, these networks are responsible for delivery of ideas and solutions to a sponsor, who usually represents a boundary-crossing coalition of different businesses or functions.

Typically, BP Amoco encourages formation of these delivery networks when the company spots a significant gap between current practices and best practices. The delivery networks are responsible for closing the gap. These delivery networks operate outside the traditional structure, because they usually aren't tied to a particular department, function, or office. Although they may receive more direction and are more directly accountable than some of the UBS networks we've described elsewhere, they still qualify as cross-functional networks with implementation responsibilities.

In every organization, experts exist who can provide the company with potentially better ways to get things done than by using the standard operating procedure. To take advantage of this resource, the wisdom network must recognize that it has implementation options and do everything possible to take advantage of the inherent talent of the members in the network, and use that ability to implement new and better ways to get things done.

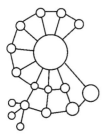

CHAPTER 10

Step 8: Performance Evaluation—Create Unconventional Measures

How do you measure the performance and value of a wisdom network that is essentially operating off the grid? Unlike teams that are part of the organizational structure, wisdom networks should not be assessed by using traditional measures. The goal is to extend organizational intelligence into wisdom; however, by placing boundaries around how wise you expect a network to be, you limit its potential. To impose goals, deadlines, and performance reviews on a network would be to devolve it from a wisdom network into a project team. This doesn't mean that you should ignore traditional measures when looking at the contributions of wisdom networks; rather, you need to integrate unconventional measures into the mix. These measures will not, of course, mimic those you use routinely, since networks provide value in new and often unorthodox ways.

Although wisdom networks can produce positive results quickly and directly, their sustainable value may emerge in a slower, less direct fashion. An idea can flow from a person through a wisdom network, be fleshed out as a leadership team gets wind of it and starts talking about it, and eventually spur a strategic adjustment that saves the company millions of dollars. If months or even years pass between the birth of the idea and its implementation, however, it's easy to forget where it originated.

Wisdom networks can be measured by answering the following question: How does organizational wisdom translate into real value?

Understand the Value of Networks

No matter their magnet topics, all networks share a singular goal of increasing profit. This is the no-brainer nature of business.

Like any other team, department, or group in a company, the ability to hit this goal is paramount, and measures should be set with this goal in mind. Wisdom networks create value in various ways. Before we talk about how to measure their value with respect to increasing profit, we'll explore five ways that wisdom networks add value:

1. Provide leadership with fresh perspectives and thought-provoking strategic concepts

Just as kings relied on wise men for counsel, CEOs rely on the wise men and women in these networks for expert advice and ideas that they won't receive anywhere else. Whether because of the hierarchical nature of organizations or human nature, leaders tend to surround themselves with people who share their way of thinking about business. As valuable as this can be in facilitating implementation strategies and moving quickly toward consensus, this homogeneity narrows leadership's perspective.

Wisdom networks add value by broadening this perspective. A diverse group of experts focused on magnet business topics will naturally view the issues in a different light than a more homogeneous, hierarchical team. Their separation from the formal structure and politics of the organization, too, provides them with a certain intellectual freedom that yields fresh insights.

At UBS, for instance, a wisdom network composed of multiple leaders from different business units was able to look at clients more holistically than an individual leader could across the same group of businesses. Network members were able to see that opportunities existed for cross-selling among business units—something that had never before been apparent from within any single business unit. For instance, sharing an understanding of certain client preferences across two different service functions helped both units to generate additional business with those clients, as well as increased client satisfaction in UBS for being able to best meet their needs. More than that, the wisdom network fostered a cross-selling consciousness among UBS leadership that filtered down to various other business leaders and teams.

Admittedly, measuring this positive impact is not always easy, but as we will discuss, it can be done.

2. Produce new methods and approaches that network members can take back to and apply in their own functions

Network participants frequently discover new ways to solve problems or capitalize on opportunities that arise in their jobs. Sometimes, this is the result of suggestions from other experts about how they handled similar situations; at other times, the wisdom network comes up with a plan or concept that is directly relevant to an issue an individual's function is confronting.

In either case, applying the wisdom that comes out of the network to a specific functional issue often produces immediate, measurable results. In other instances, however, measurement can be difficult because a member may simply have used an idea that came out of a discussion (not a formal recommendation) and implemented it. As a result, there is no paper trail or other way to document the contribution of the wisdom network to this new, effective program or process.

3. Act as change catalysts

Change can always be traced to a provocative idea, one that suggests possibilities and approaches that were never considered before or never taken seriously. A gathering of diverse experts is capable of finding ways around seemingly unmovable obstacles or bringing up viable alternatives to what were thought to be black-or-white choices.

This is another area that is difficult to measure, because change can be incremental and cumulative, so it is difficult to know what catalyzed the change in the first place. At the same time, companies that are paying attention to what goes on in wisdom networks can get a sense of how network discussions are catalyzing and facilitating change. At UBS, it was very clear that the wisdom network helped to support the company's approach to cross-selling opportunities identified and supplied through different business units.

4. Offer additional resources to help with change

In progressive organizations today, everyone is responsible for innovation. People are encouraged to think out of the box, to take risks, and to look for cutting-edge solutions. People's ability to be innovative, however, is constrained by their circumstances. Most employees find it difficult to think out of the box because their jobs tightly box in their thinking. They rarely interact with other functions on a meaningful level and have so many tasks and responsibilities that they lack the time to explore ideas that deviate too far from the norm.

Wisdom networks are great sources for innovative ideas, and people in companies quickly learn to draw on the daring thinking of diverse experts. Wisdom networks are a company's private think tanks. The discussions that go on in networks generally range far and wide. They lack the constraints of a typical team discussion, and the diverse experts push each other harder and further than they would be pushed in their day jobs. The result is an increase in innovative thinking around magnet business topics.

The members themselves often have resources at their command that can be made available to help in implementing network ideas.

5. Solve problems and capitalize on opportunities when everyone else is stuck

In most organizations, an artificial limit is imposed on the depth and breadth of ideas produced. When facing significant problems or opportunities, this limitation can be a serious issue because people can easily become stuck. When people are able to kick ideas around only with people from the same function or team, they produce only a certain number of ideas before they get stuck or start repeating themselves. The limitation is lifted when people from different groups get together in wisdom networks and cross horizontal and vertical boundaries in search of answers. They can help people overcome obstacles and get out of ruts, providing fresh thinking that may solve a problem more effectively than standard operating procedure.

In this way, wisdom networks can be measured on their ability to move groups forward when they previously were stuck.

Anecdotal Evidence: How to Collect It

Given the five ways wisdom networks add value, it makes sense to create ways to measure them. Some of the measures can be conventional, and you'll discover a clear link between wisdom network activities and positive organizational outcomes. Some measures must be unconventional, though. Measuring a wisdom network as a change catalyst or its contributions to leadership vision and values can be a challenge. Therefore, anecdotal evidence is the best measure.

By anecdotal, we're suggesting that network champions gather evidence from the stakeholders—the internal and external customers—who benefit in some way from wisdom network activities. By conducting and recording interviews with these stakeholders as well as noting the linkages between wisdom network ideas and positive outcomes, the value of networks can be ascertained.

Some of you may wonder if all this is necessary. Why gather anecdotal evidence when wisdom networks clearly produce at least some tangible evidence of their effectiveness? As we've indicated throughout, most organizations have skeptics who question knowledge management in general and its specific manifestations, such as wisdom networks. Anecdotal evidence is a way to answer their questions and silence the naysayers.

In the next section, we'll look at each of the five measures and the types of questions network champions can ask to determine a network's contributions:

1. Provide leadership with fresh perspectives and thought-provoking strategic concepts

- Did the network provide you with information or ideas that changed the way you looked at a major business issue?

- Has the output of a network resulted in changes to policies or strategies?
- What specific insights or ideas from a network were useful in dealing with a crisis or making a crucial leadership decision?

2. Produce new methods and approaches that network members can take back to and apply in their own functions

- How did the network's ideas and activities benefit your function?
- Did it help a project team meet a goal?
- Did it result in an approach that you probably would not have come up with on your own?

3. Act as change catalysts

- Of the major change initiatives launched by your company recently, how many of them were affected by the work of a wisdom network?
- How has a wisdom network helped your organization change a specific process, program, policy, or procedure?
- How has a network catalyzed cultural change within your organization; what is the connection between ideas that came out of the network and how your culture is evolving?

4. Offer additional resources to help with change

- Have wisdom networks contributed to your organization's recent innovations; what specific ideas have helped to launch cutting-edge products or services?
- Do people view wisdom networks as resources for fresh thinking, creative ideas, and breakthrough concepts; do they actively request help from wisdom networks?
- Can you describe the process by which a specific wisdom network surfaced an idea that grabbed the imagination of others in the organization and resulted in an innovation that has been highly successful?

5. Solve problems and capitalize on opportunities when everyone else is stuck

- Is there a specific instance in which your group hit a dead end and a wisdom network helped provide a fresh start on a problem or opportunity?

- What has a wisdom network done to get you unstuck; did its members provide you with fresh thinking on a situation; did its experts come up with a specific response to a problem or opportunity that you successfully implemented; or did it simply give you a new way to view the situation that helped you come up with the right approach?

- Did you find that the wisdom network offered you a viable alternative to your usual approach when you got stuck; were its members able to get you unstuck relatively quickly; would you have ever come up with this approach to getting unstuck on your own?

Tangible Measures

Although anecdotal data provides compelling evidence of a wisdom network's effectiveness, supplemental direct data is also useful. It can take a while before anecdotal evidence can be compiled; in the interim, measures that are more direct offer management a barometer of what a network is doing and trying to accomplish. Networks should monitor the following three areas as they move forward:

1. Types of activities engaged in

To people who aren't part of the knowledge management process, these ad hoc groups are a mystery. They need to be informed of how time is spent so that they realize the time is well spent. To this end, networks should chart the types of meeting they have (in-person, virtual, or conference calls), how often these meetings take place, and the subjects discussed during these meetings, Members should also note conferences attended, benchmarking trips, meetings and alliances with people outside of the organization, and so on. Again, this doesn't have to be a rigorous measure— you don't need to note every meeting or every conference call made—but it should provide a general picture of what types of tasks a network is engaged in.

2. Participation levels

This is a key indicator of wisdom network viability, especially in the eyes of skeptical executives. When participation levels show a steady increase over time, it suggests that the networks are more than a flash in the pan. People are taking them seriously, and positive word of mouth is attracting new experts who may otherwise have remained hidden within a function. As wisdom networks become a force in the company, documenting this steady growth is a good measure.

Similarly, noting who is participating also communicates a great deal about the network. Are experts from a variety of functions and at various hierarchical levels becoming involved in the network? Is their involvement consistent? This, too, sends a message about whether the network is fulfilling its mandate as a forum for diverse experts.

3. Outputs

The best and easiest output to measure is an idea that emerges from the network and is immediately implemented by a project team and results in a cost savings or increased revenue. Absent this obvious measure, networks should keep track of other outputs, including white papers, sponsorship of knowledge fairs, and specific concepts and recommendations that the network feels will have value for the company.

Different organizations are going to have different ways of assessing these measures. Some may focus on a few, specific outputs they consider of greatest value while others will look at a much greater range. In addition, one company may keep formal records of these tangible measures while others take a less formal approach.

What is important, though, is keeping a record of these three areas and doing so in a standardized manner. In this way, you can compare and contrast results from different periods of time and also have a universal barometer to use with all your networks.

The following chart is a KM measurement tool that has been used very effectively at UBS. As you'll see, it was used for start-up pilot communities and reflects the initial phase in a network's development. Still, we have found that this type of tool is easily adapted to all types of networks and is quite comprehensive in the factors it measures. It also offers numerical ratings that enhance the tangibility of the assessments.

We've included the instructions that were part of the assessment when it was distributed to some UBS community leaders. Feel free to adapt these instructions to your own purposes:

Current State Assessment Guidelines

During one of the community leader's first meetings with the KM support team, the team should establish a KM baseline with the community. By gathering data from the community leader on the following questions, the support team can better understand where the community members are currently at in terms of their KM performance and where the community requires the most support.

Purpose of the Current State Questionnaire

To establish a benchmark with pilot communities regarding their knowledge management performance by reviewing current KM practices and identifying gaps among culture, process, content, and technology.

Culture: number of diverse members in the network. Diversity includes but is not limited to:

(a) country
(b) race
(c) sex
(d) skill set
(e) educational background
(f) company background

Process: the logistical engagement of network members, including but not exclusive to:

(a) conference calls

(b) virtual meetings

(c) conventions attended

(d) keynote speakers

(e) knowledge fairs held

(f) project reviews

Content: written or delivered intelligence through

(a) white papers

(b) written lessons learned

(c) adapted best practices

(d) e-mail bulletins

(e) surveys or questionnaires completed

(f) interviews or books delivered

Technology

(a) discussion threads contributed to

(b) chat (instant messaging) channels contributed to

(c) new company reports generated

(d) e-mail distribution lists contributed to

(e) virtual team workspaces created

Relevant Definitions for Current State Questionnaire

Knowledge management describes the process of engaging in activities to capture and leverage knowledge and expertise across the organization. Establishing a community is one means by which this goal might be accomplished.

The core activities of knowledge generation, capture, use, and growth are referred to collectively as *knowledge sharing* and extend within one's community, across communities, out to the broader organization, and possibly to the outside world.

Knowledge can be tacit or explicit and shared in the form of publications, exchange of subject matter expertise, mentoring and help, and/or anecdotal evidence.

Output of the Questionnaire

1. Quantitative scores for every community regarding its performance in each of the KM building blocks—culture, process, content, and technology. For example: on a rating scale of 1 to 5, 1 being the lowest or least occurred, 5 the highest, a sample score might be: Culture = 3.5; Process = 4; Content = 2; Technology = 2.
2. Qualitative data regarding KM practices will be used by the KM team to help define a community's next steps and to develop recommendations by understanding what already works or has been tried. This data also will be used to help determine potential approaches for other similar communities.

Name_____

Community _____

Current KM Practices

Assess to what extent you believe your community practices knowledge management today (1 to 5, where 1 = not at all; 5 = completely).

1. To what extent do other communities/business units (BUs) share your community's knowledge (e.g., white papers, subject matter experts [SMEs], or community members acting as reviewers)?
2. To what extent does your community leverage knowledge from other communities, SMEs, or BUs?
3. What types of knowledge are you currently sharing with others within your community, with other communities, or with other BUs (e.g., best practices, lessons learned, product knowledge, test results, industry knowledge, or other)?

KM Strategy

1. What are the key drivers (i.e., business objectives) of your community?

2. What are the key KM objectives of your community?

3. In general, is your community focused on:

    (a) operational efficiency/cost reduction

    (b) customer intimacy/satisfaction

    (c) improved innovation/time to market

    (d) other—if so, what?

KM Culture

1. To what extent does your community have recognition processes/incentives (e.g., rewards for publications or recognition in weekly newsletter for SME contribution) in place to encourage knowledge sharing?

2. Describe any recognition processes/incentives you have in place to acknowledge members who contribute to the network's objectives.

3. To what extent does your community have defined roles and responsibilities established for members (e.g., champion, facilitator, secretary, and so on)?

KM Process

1. To what extent do you have metrics (e.g., number of contributions or number of publications) established to track knowledge sharing that takes place within or through your community? (1 to 5, where 1 = not at all; 5 = completely)

2. If you do track, what specific metrics do you use (e.g., number of people accessing information, how often a document is reused, or number of contributions)?

3. How defined is the process for managing knowledge in your community (e.g., the cycle from creating knowledge through to shar-

ing it; through to applying it; through to updating it)? (1 to 5 where 1 = not at all; 5 = extremely)

KM Content

1. To what extent do you have publication criteria (e.g., version control, review process, and required approvals) defined within your community? (1 to 5, where 1 = not at all; 5 = completely)

2. How many written pieces of knowledge has your network created (e.g., white papers, lessons learned, best practices, project reviews, and so on)?

3. How many written pieces of knowledge has your network collected from outside sources that have been reviewed and endorsed by your network SMEs?

KM Technology

Collaboration Tools:

1. What tools do you currently use to share knowledge within or through your community? For each tool used, indicate how effective the tools are and how important they are to your community (1 to 5, where 1 = not at all; 5 = extremely):

Tool	How effective are the tools you are currently using? (1–5)	How important is the tool to your community? (1–5)
a. Face-to-face meetings		
b. Virtual meetings		
c. Virtual team workspaces (e.g., MS Sharepoint, Eroom, etc.)		
d. Instant messaging		
e. E-mail		
f. Conference calls/voice mail		

g. Shared computer
   drives, shared
   e-mail folders, etc.

h. Other?

Content Management Tools:

2. What tools do you currently use for content management purposes? For each tool used, indicate how effective the tools are and how important they are to your community (1 to 5, where 1 = not at all; 5 = extremely):

Functionality	Tool Name	How effective are the tools you are currently using? (1–5)	How important is (or will be) the functionality listed to the growth and success of your community? (1–5)
a. Document storage			
b. Document management/work flow (e.g., version control, approval process, etc.)			
c. Document retrieval			
d. Search capabilities			
e. Work flow			
f. Other?			

Community Specific Tools:

3. Do you have any technology specific to your community? If so, please list the functionality provided, the name of the tool, its effectiveness, and the functional importance to the success of your community.

All these measures are going to look somewhat different company to company, so there is no set standard. There is a great value in being able to compare and contrast the knowledge behavior of your networks, as such comparisons will yield great insight in how to make them better. Since organizational cultures, business goals, and types of informal networks vary from company to company, the key is to begin to capture metrics consistently across them all, and measure both their success and failure against the metrics, building a benchmark to use for help in developing future networks with increasing success. What is perhaps most instructive, however, is that many companies can incorporate both tangible and intangible measures into their community measurement process quite successfully, and use these measures to exponentially increase the effectiveness of their networks.

Earlier, we referred to DaimlerChrysler's extensive community-building efforts and how the company's tech clubs helped to draw technical experts from different areas into these informal networks. Daimler-Chrysler uses a measurement system that on a quarterly basis assesses communities for the following factions:

- Levels of activity
- Impact on traditional business metrics
- Contributions to business goals
- Satisfaction of members
- Contributions to enhanced reputation of the organization

Using everything from surveys of community members to data analysis of how a community's recommendation has impacted a business goal, DaimlerChrysler has been able to regularly track these tangible measures to determine the value added by their communities, creating guidelines that new networks can follow to increase their chances of becoming wise.

The company has also been testing ways to track intangible measures, using storytelling and anecdotes to assess the impact of the communities on the organization. Through such a proven method of passing on wisdom and by encouraging community participants to talk about their experiences, they have been able to determine how people rely on their communities as resources for expertise when they face tough problems or great business opportunities.

Self-Measurement and Giving Credit Where Credit Is Due

As useful as measures are for the organization, they are perhaps even more valuable for members of the wisdom networks themselves. They, too, need a way to determine if they've been successful and to know they will receive credit for their hard work outside of the formal business structure. To that end, wisdom network participants should be allowed to create their own measures, which are endorsed and validated by their peers in the network. Specifically, they need to clarify what it is that their peers value about their contributions. Peer accreditation is a highly underrated, underutilized measure of a person's effectiveness, and wisdom networks are an ideal setting to put this measure into practice.

This issue can become complex, depending on what the wisdom network is working on. Consider a cross-selling example. An expert salesperson who is a member of the network knows that in his day job, if he makes X dollars worth of sales, he will receive Y dollars in compensation. Although perhaps not expecting direct compensation from his participation in the wisdom network, he still expects his continued participation to be rewarded in some way. He is motivated by what he stands to gain from being in the network and therefore should understand how he will benefit.

This can be a dicey issue when people from different departments and functions are all working on the same project. Who receives credit when the idea becomes a genuine success? Since the idea may benefit one network member's function more than another's or not benefit another member's department at all, how is each one to be recognized?

Wisdom network participants should determine at the start of their efforts what they feel a reasonable goal for the network should be, both for themselves and for the network. Also, they should give thought to the type of peer credit they are willing to accord those who deserve it. Management should ensure that recognition isn't directly in cash, but should certainly have a positive impact on the participants' careers. Perhaps they should receive certain work opportunities because of meeting their goals. Perhaps they should be given the chance to form another wisdom network on a related topic in which they have great interest.

The worst-possible scenario occurs when a wisdom network comes up with a terrific idea, which is translated into a cost-saving or revenue-enhancing program, and some members feel that, while some of their fellow network members benefited from the idea, they did not. Ultimately, this causes friction that tears the network apart. This can easily cause people to become resentful and never want to participate in a network again.

This scenario is more likely to occur if the network members fail to think about and discuss how they will each benefit if they come up with a breakthrough concept. When these issues aren't thought through at the start of the process, people are often disappointed and angry at the end, even when they have been successful. Therefore, the network members should reach a consensus on what they believe would be a successful outcome to their work and what each of them wants to get out of it if the outcome is achieved.

Typical rewards and recognition might include the following:

- The opportunity to apply the new methodology in their own department

- The chance to launch the network anew on an issue of greater relevance to their particular function

- Recognition from the CEO that is communicated to their bosses that they made a major contribution to a major business concern

- Participation in the elite task force charged with implementing the wisdom network's idea

- Permission to attend an international conference on a topic related to the topic on which the wisdom network was focused

Creating measures for success and linking them to positive outcomes for members of the network helps to build self-sustaining wisdom networks. These networks aren't like traditional teams with predefined objectives or task forces that dissolve once the mission is achieved. These networks must be self-renewing, and the experts who compose them must be motivated to continue to devote their time and energy to them. These are voluntary positions, and organizations should be aware of the real danger of experts dropping out because the experience was less than satisfying. Certainly, network participants will take satisfaction from the intellectual challenge and chance to work on pet projects and topics of personal interest. If, however, they believe their effort wasn't appreciated or that favoritism caused some network members to receive more credit than others, they will grow disenchanted with the process and drop out of networks.

When network members are allowed to establish fair measures for success and appropriate recognition for that success, they are much more likely to be enthusiastic and highly energized participants, which are key ingredients that sustain and evolve networks.

Flexible Measures

We have discussed a wide variety of measures because many companies make the mistake of having no measures for their ad hoc groups and communities, thereby failing to provide these groups or management with any way to judge their progress or effectiveness. In these cases, the lack of measures often turns the skeptic's view into a self-fulfilling prophecy: Because there are no measures for effectiveness, no one believes that these groups are truly effective.

It's easy to understand why metrics are often ignored. Knowledge management executives rightly recognize that these ad hoc groups are different and should not be judged by the same standards as more formal teams. Erring on the side of no measures, however, can cause just as many problems as imposing standard measures.

Rather than no measurements, we recommend keeping them flexible and loose. Organizations make them inflexible and tightly controlling by doing the following:

- Locking wisdom networks into hard and fast delivery dates
- Giving them specific objectives and a framework in which they must operate
- Having them report to the head of a function and file regular reports
- Evaluating them based on ROI—insisting that the time of the experts plus whatever financial investment is made must produce a greater financial return

A wisdom network's value is diluted by these controls. The network members' intellectual freedom, ability to operate in a parallel universe (to the corporate structure), license to work at their own pace in their own ways, and separation from the politics and bureaucratic red tape of the larger system are compromised when traditional measures are imposed.

The key, therefore, is to strike a balance between no measures and unconventional measures. We recognize that each wisdom network is different; one may be working on a topic where anecdotal evidence of progress and success suffices, while another may be addressing a magnet business topic where immediate, measurable results are essential. A neophyte wisdom network in a company that is relatively new to the knowledge management arena will probably require different measures from a veteran network in a company well versed in KM principles. So, every situation is different, but the rule should be that measures are to be kept relatively loose and unconventional, but evolving.

This rule is especially important if you want to build self-sustaining wisdom networks—that is, ones that grow in response to changing magnet business topics. Unlike traditional teams and task forces, these networks have a life cycle all their own. It is a life cycle that we're still learning about since these networks are still in their infancy, even at companies like UBS. What we know, though, is that there is an ebb and flow to their existence, periods when they are much more prominent and active than others.

What typically happens is that when a magnet topic becomes a top priority for a company, the wisdom network tends to meet often, have high attendance at their meetings, and produce all sorts of outputs through white papers, project recommendations, and so on. At other times, however, a given network's expertise on a subject is a lower priority. During these dormant or less active periods, the wisdom network members are devoting more time to their day jobs and less to the network. Consequently, their output through the wisdom network is less.

Companies need to be careful not to come to false conclusions about these networks during dormant periods. They should not assume that because activity has diminished, they are no longer contributing value. They need to be aware that it is perfectly natural for a network to take a backseat for a while, since there are periods when some wisdom is more important to the company than others. It is valuable, therefore, to create an unconventional measure that communicates to leadership that a given network's expertise is less critical at a certain time, because it prevents management from becoming upset with the lack of contributions of a network at this particular moment. Just as important, organizations should be aware when a network's brand of expertise is essential, and that these are the times when the company should engage the network, request assistance, and provide whatever additional support is necessary. This isn't that complicated, but it does take a certain awareness of off-the-grid networks, their composition and expertise, and how their wisdom dovetails with the company's pressing business needs.

It is obvious, then, that flexibility is crucial because wisdom is not always easily measured. Networks often make recommendations and produce new concepts. They may suggest courses of action that strike some in the organization as too risky or too unorthodox. They may also step on toes with their recommendations, upsetting departments and functions within the organization because they are not bound by organizational politics. Wisdom can produce ingenious ideas, but ingenuity is a threat in some people's eyes.

One wisdom network in a high-tech company, for instance, was composed of financially savvy experts from different functions who were looking for ways to reduce costs, because the company had taken on a high burden of debt with a recent acquisition. For several months, the company had been relying on a task force composed largely of people from the financial function to come up with a cost-reduction plan, but their conventional ideas struck leadership as flawed.

The wisdom network's recommendation was anything but conventional. The group proposed reducing the company's marketing function to a small, administrative staff and outsourcing their responsibilities to an advertising agency and a direct marketing firm. Based on their expertise, they had determined that the marketing function, which had been critical in the company's early success, had become bloated and inefficient in recent years. Still, it was a politically powerful function, and this recommendation set off a firestorm of protest from the company's top marketing executives.

Even though the high-tech company didn't implement this recommendation, it did adapt it and was able to achieve a considerable savings by trimming some jobs from the marketing department and reorganizing it. More important, the CEO and other top executives did not measure the wisdom network's performance according to conventional terms. They did not dismiss the group's ideas because they created political controversy or deem the network impractical because the ideas couldn't be fully implemented. Instead, they talked to various functional heads about the network's recommendation and found that almost all of them thought the network had been extraordinarily insightful in its ideas and that the ideas had merit. In other words, they were able to measure the network with an open mind.

Improved Strike Ratio: Going Beyond Peak Performance

We're using the term *strike ratio* both literally and figuratively. Literally, it means the number of hits you get based on rockets fired. If you fire ten rockets and get only three hits, an improved strike ratio may be five hits out of ten. In an organization, this translates easily into sales, where you may have one hundred prospects at any given moment and your conversion rate to sales is 12 percent. A strike rate of 20 percent, therefore, would be a significant improvement.

Figuratively, it simply means increasing effectiveness given the resources at hand. How can a company increase overall productivity from its current employees without additional hires? How can the company's quality process reduce defects per part without investing a lot more money in the quality control process? How can it increase the retention rate for key employees without spending a lot more money on salaries and bonuses?

These are key measures where an improved strike ratio for any given business target is contingent on the right information and ideas. Most of the time, people are operating at peak capacity or close to it. Salespeople who have one hundred prospects are doing everything they know how to do to increase their conversion percentages, but despite achieving good percentages, they can't move significantly beyond a certain level. Most people in organizations reach peak levels that can be exceeded only with a significant increase in financial expenditures—or with an influx of wisdom.

We've observed that wisdom networks are increasing people's ability to improve performance and achieve other significant gains by using the same resources they had before. For instance, a salesperson with one hundred prospects joins a wisdom network that is talking about establishing cross-connecting relationships with other salespeople in different departments and offices around the world. Through the discussion, this salesperson realizes that she, like other salespeople, is convinced that her colleagues in separate areas have no knowledge that might help her. Thus, little sharing of information and ideas between salespeople in different groups occurs. The wisdom network, however, concludes that each salesperson has developed best practices and contacts that can benefit other sales groups if a mutual exchange occurs. Using this wisdom, the salesperson is able to increase her conversion rate.

It is important, therefore, for management to be aware of instances when a wisdom network could increase strike ratios. This is one more piece of anecdotal evidence that demonstrates the value of a wisdom network, and one that could readily turn into factual evidence. When a group or team makes a significant improvement in an area, or if one fails to achieve a significant objective, the lesson should be captured and reused. Of course, there are often several catalysts, but it may well be that an idea or discussion in a wisdom network led to the outcome, and this should be noted and used as a measure of the network's worth to the organization.

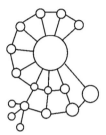

CHAPTER 11

Growing Pains: The Care, Feeding, and Evolution of Wisdom Networks

Let us assume that you have helped create wisdom networks within your organization, following the advice we've provided. You have reached the point where management recognizes networks as valuable resources that are contributing to the achievement of business goals. No doubt, some people in the organization are still skeptical about their value, and the participation level of experts may not be as high as you would like. Nonetheless, networks have established a foothold, and you see great things ahead for them as they gain greater acceptance and support.

A question, of course, is how to help wisdom networks, and the organization, to achieve truly great things that reach far beyond expectations. Another is how do you sustain these networks after they've been established. More to the point, how do you help these networks sustain themselves? How do you make sure they don't become the flavor of the month, to be replaced by some other KM approach next month or next year? How do you help them grow and move to the next level in their evolution?

To answer these questions, you need to understand the natural movement of wisdom networks over time and ways you can contribute to this movement.

The Ideal Scenario: Wisdom Network Growth and Development

Figure 11-1 depicts the ideal path of wisdom networks as they grow and mature.

Certainly, not every ad hoc group that is born survives to this point, but assuming that organizations adopt the principles we've suggested, the odds are good that a pilot or beginning network will grow beyond its early localized status and bring in experts who represent a variety of areas throughout the organization. Similarly, over a period of time, its ideas will be not merely innovative but transformational, and as the network matures it will have a positive impact on business goals and its wisdom will be leveraged across the corporation to be used in many different ways.

To facilitate this growth and ever-widening impact, companies must identify, encourage, and recognize these groups. We've discussed different ways management can do this, but here we want to look at things from a time-based perspective so that leaders know what they should do as networks expand and increase their impact.

Figure 11-1 indicates three responsibilities of the network champion or anyone else in supportive leadership positions in the early phase of a network. Although these responsibilities may seem obvious now that you've read this book, they can be easily overlooked in real business life. Many organizations never identify their informal networks and are surprised when they learn of their existence and expertise. To make sure that networks in early stages continue to grow and develop, therefore, be sure to do these identification tasks, especially resolving start-up problems. It may be that the focus of the network is slightly off kilter—that is, it's not addressing key business goals or it is lacking the resources it needs to move forward in a meaningful way. Don't take your networks for granted and assume they can resolve all their problems without your assistance.

As a network solidifies its presence, leadership must provide it with continuing encouragement. This may mean changing the type of support

Figure 11-1. How to focus support for your networks.

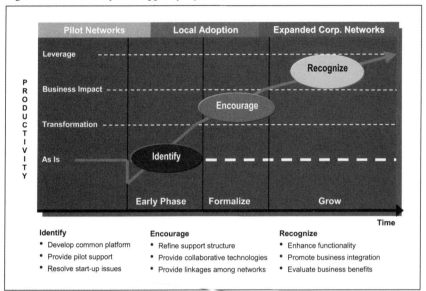

Identify	Encourage	Recognize
• Develop common platform	• Refine support structure	• Enhance functionality
• Provide pilot support	• Provide collaborative technologies	• Promote business integration
• Resolve start-up issues	• Provide linkages among networks	• Evaluate business benefits

it receives based on its growing stature and impact. It may mean connecting one network to another if the two are working on similar business goals. Leaders are in the best position to recognize and capitalize on potential synergies between and among networks. Finally, as networks grow and expand their impact, they must be recognized in all senses of this word. In this way, organizations can keep networks on their natural trajectory and allow them to be propelled by the power of their wisdom.

The Proof of the Pudding: Countering Resistance

Even if some wisdom networks contribute breakthrough concepts that result in revenue-generating innovations or perhaps in the elimination of huge cost redundancies, a certain percentage of the workforce—from young at skill and new employees to veteran hands and senior executives—will resist sharing knowledge with people in other functions and hierarchical organizational levels. If you don't address this issue, it can prove fatal to wisdom networks and create potentially dangerous cultural trends that will prevent the company from changing when it must in order to remain competitive.

As we've discussed, the only way you can win skeptics over is by showing them how a wisdom network will help them do their jobs better, faster, and cheaper. This means sharing case histories that demonstrate how wisdom networks have helped other people achieve significant business objectives. It means learning about the obstacles and opportunities they face in their jobs and explaining how and why wisdom networks may help them to overcome these obstacles and capitalize on these opportunities. It means sharing the hard lessons learned when ideas or networks fail, leaving egos at the door, trusting network colleagues, and making an even greater commitment to address the magnet topic.

Once wisdom networks have gained a foothold, such as in the companies we've discussed, they offer tangible proof that they have value. Wisdom network champions, however, must actively discuss and argue for these networks. If wisdom network champions assume that a single success from a single wisdom network will naturally win over all the naysayers, they are mistaken.

When Ideas Don't Work: Overcoming Failure

At the same time, don't assume that one wisdom network failure will doom the entire process. Just as it may take a few new ideas to hit on one that actually pays off, failed ideas coming out of wisdom networks will certainly outnumber the successes. Although people are disappointed when a wisdom network doesn't deliver a terrific idea that has a hugely positive outcome, especially after earlier wisdom network successes have conditioned them to expect great things, they recognize that no one can hit home runs every time at bat. This is especially true if the wisdom network put in a lot of effort, did a significant amount of research, thought through the idea, and came up with something that seemed new and powerful. The process itself reveals the great potential of wisdom networks and provides an opportunity for codification for future efforts, so that even failures can be impressive learning experiences.

Keep Your Eye on the Prize: Maintaining Focus

It is much more likely that the wisdom network system will start crumbling though, if the networks become detached from the magnet business topics.

If their work doesn't address key business issues, solve major problems, and produce big improvements, people will lose interest. When wisdom networks start drifting into marginal topics and issues of parochial self-interest, they cease to be a force for innovation and growth in a company.

UBS, for instance, is in the process of refocusing the work of some of its various business networks and support communities so that they will drive business change in each of the company's core product lines. It's not that UBS's various groups weren't addressing key business topics previously, but it takes constant vigilance, refining of focus, and redoubling of effort to maintain and strengthen the connection between wisdom networks and business improvement.

At UBS and some of the other companies we've discussed, this focus is a result of positive, distinctive attitudes about knowledge sharing from the CEO on down. Let's examine the nature of this attitude and the importance of spreading and inculcating it as wisdom networks grow.

An Organizational Ethos: Knowledge Sharing as a Right

When sharing knowledge is merely a task, a responsibility, or an obligation, innovation rarely takes place. Wisdom networks that operate in cultures where people feel forced to exchange knowledge often fail to thrive. Instead, they go through the motions of knowledge exchanges. Groups talk about topics and can help to codify knowledge, but the free and dynamic exchanges that we've described don't happen. People hold back ideas or fear sharing too much. In addition, cultures like these tend to shoot down ideas that wisdom networks produce.

When this happens, rather than taking an objective approach to these networks, management views their contributions with a jaundiced eye. They suspect that the ideas will be too "far out" and look for excuses to turn them down or prevent their implementation. Even if a few wisdom networks are able to get projects implemented, many participants become discouraged by the rejections and drop out.

When we talk about an organizational ethos in which knowledge sharing is a right, we mean that experts feel that as part of the organization they are entitled to find ways to communicate their information and opinions to others about a topic that excites them. When this is a right to which they are entitled, they don't have to confine their knowledge sharing to only job-specific issues. Instead, they volunteer information and concepts when they believe it will help others do their jobs better or achieve key business goals.

When they come up with a great idea, they don't say to themselves: "I can't talk about this because it's outside of my area of responsibility" or "Maybe I should keep this to myself because I can use it to help my career." As a right, knowledge sharing is something that is exercised at an individual employee's discretion, not at the organization's insistence, so it becomes a very powerful motivational factor.

To keep wisdom networks alive and well, leaders must create cultures where people are eager to pass expertise to others, where brainstorming across boundaries is an integral part of the work routine, and where an expert in one function is able to tell a person in another function how something he or she discovered might be of benefit to the other group. It may seem like a small thing, but when leaders create this sharing consciousness—when people believe it is their right as an employee to exchange knowledge—wisdom networks become, and remain, a significant force.

Here are some ways that companies can safeguard the right of experts to share what they know:

1. Make sure that at least some members of the management team are viewed as leaders when it comes to knowledge sharing

Wisdom networks will become endangered if their champion in the management ranks leaves and no one of a similar mind-set replaces this person. Knowledge can be easily lost through attrition, making it critical that companies be alert for growing knowledge gaps when key people leave the company. In a typical management team, some members will be indifferent or even opposed to wisdom networks. Without support from leadership, wisdom networks can become marginal, or nonexistent, rather than an integral part of the organization.

For this reason, it is wise for companies to keep knowledge management skills in mind when they recruit top people. This doesn't mean they need to have a knowledge management officer, but rather that in the past they have demonstrated an appreciation for knowledge sharing and exchange, and perhaps participated in the process of community and network development in some way. For example, they may have written white papers on the subject or led seminars and conferences on related topics. What you want to avoid are situations where no one in management has any skill or interest in knowledge management.

Instead of bringing in people from the outside, organizations can also make knowledge management a competency for its leaders. Job specifications for top management positions should include at least some understanding of KM principles. Ideally, participating in a community of interest or some other ad hoc group would be considered a positive experience for all leaders.

2. Create an ongoing corporate discussion about information, ideas, knowledge, and wisdom

In some companies, knowledge management issues are out of sight and out of mind. There might be wisdom networks, but they operate in literal and figurative back rooms, and the majority of employees never think about what they do or how they contribute beyond their immediate jobs to the broader organizational goals. Because these wisdom networks operate outside of the traditional structures, without support and active endorsement of leaders, they are not noticed by most people and their achievements are known only to a relative few.

For this reason, organizations should look for opportunities to create talk—and even debate—about wisdom networks, communities of interest, and other forums for knowledge exchange. This can mean everything from white papers on the subject, internal conferences and workshops, websites that spotlight the activities of these communities, online discussion threads, and more informal discussions around the watercooler during breaks or over lunches. Ideally, this will ensure that not only will the work of wisdom networks be understood and their accomplishments acknowledged but also that a shared sense of network ownership emerges throughout the company, establishing networks' value among a broad cross section of employees.

3. Let sharing evolve naturally

This is a more subtle point than the other two, but equally important. Sometimes, wisdom network supporters are overly enthusiastic about the knowledge management process and tell experts that "you have to tell people what you know about X" or they insist that savvy veterans mentor young up-and-comers by sharing those secrets that keep them where they are.

No one likes to be told what to do, especially if you're an expert or a savvy veteran. Push these individuals to share and they will do so only grudgingly. They will make cosmetic efforts and pretend that they're going along with the program, but they're thinking to themselves, "This too shall pass."

And it will! If people are forced to participate in communities or to share their knowledge in other forums, wisdom networks will disintegrate. The last thing you want to do is to conscript experts and force them to be wisdom network "volunteers." Networks thrive on the enthusiasm, motivation, and energy of people committed to learning and helping others to learn, and if the process is an imposition rather than an invitation, it won't work.

At UBS and other companies, people ask others to share what they know. They give them the opportunity and the freedom to do so in ways that make sense to them. It is not "all knowledge for all people." Experts are not asked to share everything with everyone, but to determine where a particular piece of information or area of knowledge might make a significant impact on business goals if they pass it on. The attitude is always that this is their right to exercise as they see fit, and they control what they share. As a result, people don't view knowledge sharing through networks as onerous tasks but as voluntary activities in which they want to participate—activities with real rewards and benefits that are sustainable.

4. Resist the urge to control wisdom networks or turn them into project teams

In companies where knowledge management is entrenched and wisdom networks proliferate, senior management may perceive opportunities to get more out of these networks by having greater control of them. This is a misperception. The more that networks are thought of as part of the system and therefore in need of regulation and control, and the more they are governed by the policies and processes that govern all functions, the less effective they will be. To give them a budget, to incorporate them into a department, and to give them performance objectives all turn them into just another project, department, or task force.

Therefore, don't co-opt them. As long as they exist as a separate resource, wisdom network participants will continue to exercise their right to share knowledge.

Address the Fears That Highly Successful Wisdom Networks Might Foster

When wisdom networks take off, they produce a great deal of excitement and motivation, but they can also create anxiety. As they begin making significant contributions from the standpoint of innovation and as groups begin relying on them for fresh ideas and insights, they can actually create issues that are a concern. Here are some of those issues most likely to surface and ways to address them effectively:

1. *People are neglecting their day jobs*

This fear can be countered by making sure everyone knows that wisdom networks are subordinate to job responsibilities. No one should be asked or permitted to abdicate their job responsibilities in favor of network participation. If they do, senior managers must make it extremely clear that daily responsibilities are, as always, the top priority. As much as people enjoy their work in communities and other ad hoc groups, they must understand that in many ways, this is an extracurricular activity, one that is encouraged but only if it brings value back to the day jobs of its members as well as positive change to the business.

What tends to diminish this fear is the way in which people find a balance between their regular jobs and their network participation. During times when their jobs are stressful and demanding, they necessarily have to limit their participation in networks or engage in them outside of the traditional business day. When the pace slackens, they can find time in between their regular job responsibilities for network activities.

People in communities should not expect management to set aside time for them to spend in their ad hoc groups. If management were to take this step, it would be taking control of the process. Admittedly, everyone is pressed for time and it is always a challenge to do everything you want in a given day. Nonetheless, we have found that most members of communities are adept at carving out the time they need because they don't separate community time from day job time. They have made the mental shift to see both activities as part of the same job. They know that their wisdom network activities will help them do their day jobs better, and so they are creative about integrating meetings and other network tasks into their routines. In some situations, they might need to find time for their networks outside of office hours, but they also capitalize on slow periods, lunches, and gaps in their schedules to devote to network goals. In this way, they do justice to both their formal and informal responsibilities.

When people prove adept at finding a satisfactory balance, fears about job neglect tend to vanish. And when it starts to become obvious that wisdom gained through the network is being applied beneficially to people's daily tasks, active support for networks begins to emerge.

Organizations shouldn't panic when these fears initially arise, since the natural forces within an organization tend to prompt people to find a good balance. The hierarchical system still keeps people accountable to their bosses and supervisors, and the rewards and recognitions systems are (and should remain) tied to their job performance.

2. The hierarchical structure will be weakened or destroyed

As wisdom networks grow more numerous and become an increasingly important part of the organization, some leaders may feel that their growth is having a negative impact on the hierarchy and the company's ability to execute. They fear that knowledge management and its associated communities and networks are flattening the structure to the point where it will become all idea makers, with no "doers" or decision makers. They watch one community of interest become five communities of practice become ten wisdom networks, and they wonder where it will stop.

There are two ways to counter this fear. First, share case histories of companies that have embraced knowledge sharing, organizational learning, and network development. The vast majority of these companies still have a strong, hierarchical structure. The growth of networks in these companies has actually solidified their traditional structures, providing an alternative to the organizational flattening some companies have chosen in order to become more innovative. To dismantle a traditional, effective hierarchy takes more than the creation of various communities and networks. It requires radical restructuring steps such as the elimination of management layers.

Second, position wisdom networks as a powerful resource to help everyone do their jobs better. Too often, ad hoc groups in companies are positioned poorly or not at all. When they are positioned poorly, they are perceived as competitors or usurpers of power. For instance, when companies create communities and give them decision-making power or authority over functional heads, they become a rival, parallel structure rather than a resource, and are rightly feared.

3. Networks will create radical, "lunatic fringe" ideas that can hurt the company or never be implemented effectively

Demystify wisdom networks and this fear will disappear. People who have never been involved in the knowledge management process or participated in even the most basic grassroots community will naturally have a fear of the unknown. One of the best ways to resolve this is by inviting them to a network meeting or sharing ideas and working methodology with them. In the vast majority of cases, once these fearful individuals are included in the loop, they become much more tolerant of wisdom networks and often become ardent network supporters, recognizing that the networks are focused on key business drivers rather than simply in it to push the envelope.

4. Networks will become forums for mundane conversation and gossip rather than exchanges of real, useful knowledge

The concern is that over time and with greater participation on the part of employees, networks will devolve rather than evolve. Instead of being composed of people with expertise and the willingness to share it, networks will include individuals who join only because they view participation as a career opportunity. Rather than being good networkers with strong contacts, they operate as "nodes of one." They are negligent about bringing fresh ideas and information to discussions, don't take meetings seriously, and keep discussions at safe levels instead of pushing into the realm of new and exciting ideas.

Wisdom networks should be self-regulating, and if they are, this won't happen. What we've found is that the majority of members discourage others from remaining members if they don't participate, regularly attend meetings, and contribute ideas that add value. They have such a commitment to the network and believe so strongly in its purpose that they do not suffer dilettantes gladly. There is no overt shunning or blackballing of nonparticipants, but active members make their expectations known. They communicate that membership in a dynamic community isn't for everyone, and that some people might want to consider whether they have the time or energy to devote to the community. Sometimes, people join communities thinking they are one thing and are dismayed when they realize they are something else. They eventually drop out, feeling more comfortable devoting all of their time to their day jobs.

For its part, management should not allow wisdom networks to be viewed as career stepping-stones. Although participation in a network should be a positive mark on an individual's record, it should not become a job specification for a managerial position or an unofficial requirement for advancement.

The Role of Wisdom Networks in a Global, Virtual Environment

We believe wisdom networks are going to grow by leaps and bounds in the coming years because they meet emerging needs. Most obviously, they are an optimum way to maximize the value of knowledge that exists within every company. As organizations become larger, more diverse, and more global, their knowledge necessarily becomes more fragmented. The need for greater specialization creates stronger silos. Knowledge becomes lodged in organizational corners rather than shared across boundaries.

Wisdom networks provide the perfect vehicle to free this knowledge and transform it into real value. By their very nature, they allow an exchange of knowledge that crosses all types of boundaries. Sophisticated communication technology permits people to meet in various virtual forums. From informal corporate chat rooms to more formal online forums, people from all over the globe can get together and share stories, lessons learned, and best practices.

We have also found that wisdom networks are an antidote to information overload. Everyone is inundated with market trend studies and customer data, with financial reports and economic surveys. So much information crosses our desks so fast that we don't know how to make sense of it, or to determine what is wheat and what is chaff. Because of sophisticated information technology, we're able to shoot this data to ten or one hundred or one thousand people in one quick e-mail. Although it's nice to have access to this information instantly, it's not so nice when it is coming at us with incredible speed and volume.

Wisdom networks offer the opportunity to share a wide range of experiences and make sense of that information. In most companies, someone in the London office doesn't know what someone in the New York office has discovered about a process or strategy. Even if they were to communicate regularly on business matters, they lack a forum where they can move beyond the narrow framework of their job-related discussions and really share what they know.

Freed from the restraints of job-specific discussions, one of them might discuss how he attempted to implement a new policy dictated by the central office and found that it worked only if certain unofficial tweaks were employed. The other individual might talk about how she too found the policy untenable as is and that she tweaked it using a different technique. In a global company where corporate headquarters tries to standardize methods and processes, local offices invariably run into problems, and they need this type of alternative forum to exchange information about successes, failures, and best practices. Invariably, this commingling of diverse expertise will result in a new and more effective approach that can not only help local offices do their jobs better but also provide the entire global operation with a new and improved methodology.

Finally, one of the hallmarks of wisdom networks is trust, and trust is essential in an increasingly global, virtual world. In the past, trust was built through personal interaction, but in today's environment, people who work together are often separated by thousands of miles. Even when they are separated by only a few floors, so much business is conducted on websites and via e-mail that it is difficult to build trust the old-fashioned way.

Wisdom networks facilitate the building of trusting relationships because they operate outside the functional, hierarchical realm. They provide new means to establish trust. Politics and job competitiveness are absent, allowing people to drop their guard and be themselves. Even if interactions take place in virtual space and through phone conversations, participants build trust by being open and honest and sharing their hard-won knowledge of what works best. This trust allows people to take chances. They are not afraid of earning a black mark in someone's book because they suggest an approach that may strike some as radical or naive.

We have witnessed wisdom network discussions where people say things that they would never say in traditional project group or team meetings. They will speak honestly about how a leader's obstinate nature is creating a roadblock to an important new business initiative or how a function's limitations are holding the company back; they may propose outsourcing a task, which, in an ordinary corporate meeting, would cause all sorts of fireworks. In short, trust comes naturally to wisdom network participants and allows them to address issues that might otherwise be unaddressed.

It also permits them to engage in *peripheral talk*. This is a term people at Diamond Technology use to refer to conversations that take place outside of formal meetings and other structured organizational exchanges of information. These conversations are peripheral in the sense that they include observations, analysis, and ideas that generally aren't articulated during more formal exchanges because they seem off the point in some way. Within this peripheral talk, however, there exist keen insights and daring ideas that are usually lost in large, global organizations where only structured exchanges of information and ideas are captured. Wisdom networks encourage peripheral talk, shape it into business-relevant ideas, and communicate it to others in the organization.

Resist the Temptation to Control Network Evolution

Turner Construction Company is the largest commercial builder in the United States, with more than six thousand employees. In many ways, the company's knowledge management program is state of the art. Turner has integrated its learning management system and its learning content management system, giving the company a highly sophisticated way of monitoring communities of practice, creating learning paths, offering courses, and doing many other things that facilitate knowledge exchanges. In fact, as Turner put its knowledge management plan into practice, the company realized that its IT structure wouldn't support the plan, so it redesigned or replaced every computer, server, router, and switch in the company.

In addition, Turner created a knowledge-network board of executives, representing a cross section of the company, to oversee knowledge management efforts. The company also plans to install a network champion for each business unit. This person will be part of the senior business team and responsible for knowledge transfer to other business units throughout the organization.

In one sense, we applaud what Turner has accomplished. The company's leadership support for knowledge exchanges and its financial and cultural commitment is exemplary. Therefore, we don't want to suggest that the company is missing the boat. Clearly, it is doing what it believes is best to maximize the value of knowledge in the company.

What concerns us, however, is that the company's knowledge management program is so structured and so technology-driven that it may be missing out on the energy, spontaneity, and creativity that arise when people come together on their own. When informal networks emerge and develop outside of the organization's structure and have an unprecedented amount of freedom, participating experts feel that it is "their thing." They approach their topics with passion and without creative restraint, relishing the freedom from reports and rules as well as the chance to interact with an astonishingly diverse range of fellow experts. If too much structure and direction is imposed on this group, its value will be diminished.

Although we have recommended a certain amount of monitoring and support, we also advise every company to keep its networks separate from the more formal entities and free of the traditional rules of engagement in the organization. This ensures that network members can go about their network tasks in ways that are different from how they go about their functional jobs. Allowing them unprecedented freedom may seem inefficient and risky, but it is also a way to help them become a sustainable resource of increasing value.

The Next Level: What Wisdom Networks Can Become and How to Help Them Get There

UBS and other companies are just starting to tap the potential of wisdom networks. To understand why most organizations have only scratched the surface, consider the depth of knowledge that resides in a given company and how that depth is rarely plumbed. In an organization of ten thousand employees, perhaps one thousand experts exist with varying degrees of expertise. Let us further assume that only one hundred of these experts actively and consistently participate in their organization's various ad hoc communities and networks. And let us also assume that many of the ideas discussed in these communities are not captured and used because of disconnects (lack of support or champions, negative cultures, and so on) with the larger organization. Finally, we can also realistically conclude that some of these communities will be wasting considerable amounts of energy addressing nonmagnet topics—ones that are of greater interest to community members than to the organization.

As we gain experience with wisdom networks and learn how to make them function more effectively, we are bound to increase their value. Tremendous amounts of knowledge exist within every company, but much of it goes unused by the organization as a whole.

Fortunately, leaders have recognized this fact, resulting in the birth and growth of the knowledge management function. Awareness of this issue is a good start, but it is only the start. Years from now, the knowledge exchanges occurring today in even the most sophisticated wisdom networks will probably seem rudimentary. Invariably, these exchanges will produce more wisdom and become more widespread.

Perhaps the best way to glimpse the future is to look how "blogging" is used to support virtual communities that exist throughout the Internet, and what is taking place in them. Students, for instance, have formed communities around subjects they're interested in or are currently studying, which are open to anyone in the world who is willing to make a contribution. Blogs allow anyone to post information or to comment on these subjects, which everyone can see and to which anyone can respond. These are pure knowledge exchanges, and those who participate learn of cutting-edge research and potential breakthroughs, sometimes before their professors do.

In the technology realm, open source development has become a hot trend, as programming language students create blogs to share their wisdom and ideas about developing new software. They become members of virtual communities and jointly develop software that is available at no cost and that can actually be competitive with products from industry giants such as Microsoft (e.g., Linux). If someone contributes a software module that doesn't work properly, others will fix it or enhance it so that it becomes functional, thereby ensuring they can use it themselves and making it more valuable to all members.

All these virtual communities are self-sustaining and evolving. Their participants are motivated by their passion for the subject, and their focus changes as trends and interests change. People who contribute the most become stars of these online communities while those who don't contribute drop out. Different virtual communities come together and break apart in an effort to capitalize on divergent knowledge streams, and as they divide and reconnect with other groups, they resemble an evolving organism, becoming stronger and more sophisticated with each mutation.

Wisdom networks will undergo the same evolutionary cycle. The division and reformation of different networks will accelerate as industry trends shift and organizational direction follows suit. As companies become comfortable with these networks operating off the grid and as the networks become smarter about how to obtain support and resources, they will grow, expand, divide, and ultimately become more significant contributors to every area of a company's operation. They will be resources that every function turns to when they need help in a given area, and leadership will rely on them for assistance in achieving major business goals. They will also become a company's innovation engine, driving the process of idea creation.

We don't know if this future is only a year or two off or five. Obviously, different companies will reach this level at different times, and even within companies, different networks will evolve in their own time. Everyone, however, can help his or her organizations move toward this future by focusing on the following objectives:

1. Recognize the networks that exist, and work toward expanding their number

It's not that the actual number is important, but that a broad range of networks come into being in response to specific business requirements. If you have one network, you should try to find additional magnet topics that grow from one into five; if you have five, you should shoot for ten. Theoretically, at least, the more wisdom networks in operation, the more wisdom that is being mined from the company. In practice, the networks have to meet the criteria we've established; that is, they must be cross-functional, contain true experts, receive support and encouragement from leadership, have a champion, and be focused on business magnet topics. If they meet these criteria and they are expanding exponentially one-to-one as the top business topics do, your company will have a deep well of wisdom on which to draw.

2. Convert the fence straddlers

Don't waste energy trying to convince the closed-minded who will never be convinced that knowledge sharing has significant value and that wisdom networks will help shape the company's future. It is not a waste of energy, though, to focus on the fence straddlers. These open-minded individuals need to be convinced that wisdom networks are critical to the organization. If you can convince them, they will provide the type of support networks need to flourish.

UBS performed a series of interviews on employee attitudes about knowledge management, and many managers and key leaders around the globe agreed that knowledge sharing was valuable and that the right knowledge could help them excel in their jobs and also help the business excel. One manager, however, was a fence straddler. His reason was interesting. He didn't like relying on other people to come up with good ideas to help others do their jobs. He insisted, and rightly so, that it was an individual's experience and knowledge of a particular subject that landed the person the job in the first instance. The person with assigned responsibility rather than someone from "outside" would be best able to solve problems and capitalize on opportunities in his or her area, and even come up with new ideas ideally suited to his or her function. This individual suggested that a much better way of acquiring new ideas and knowledge was to have team members rotate through job training in different areas of the company and participate in job exchanges.

By engaging this person in discussions and walking him through examples of how wisdom might add value when coming from outside his area of responsibility, UBS helped this person recognize that job exchanges alone were impractical. The company also helped him to understand that relying on wisdom networks would not compromise anyone's ability to do his or her job but would provide additional resources that could potentially help him or her do it even better. Finally, UBS communicated that sometimes coming up with an entirely new advantageous business model from within an existing model might be extremely difficult without objective input from outsiders. After these discussions, this fence straddler soon became a convert, realizing that all these means of increasing wisdom might be valuable vehicles in helping to provide competitive advantage.

3. Honor expertise as the ultimate core competency

This final point may seem self-evident, but in most companies, knowledge, savvy, know-how, and other synonyms for expertise usually aren't viewed as a competency. Too often, knowledge is taken for granted. People who are experts achieve a certain status within their function, but their expertise isn't seen as something that can be leveraged.

People with true expertise, however, should occupy the same status as wise men in ancient cultures. They should be encouraged to share what they know and supported in that sharing at every turn. Experts in all areas of the company should be given ample opportunity to meet and put their combined knowledge together. There should be a general understanding that what they know is directly proportional to what they share and how they share it. Consequently, the organization should bend over backward to find ways for them to offer their knowledge to others, and to receive other experts' knowledge in return.

Perhaps more than anything else, revering knowledge and its exchange will fuel the growth and increase the value of wisdom networks, helping them reach a level that few have accomplished and many only dream about.

Steve Benton is an executive director of information technology at financial services giant UBS Investment Bank. He leads a global business service in knowledge management and has been with the firm for the past nineteen years and in the information technology field for nearly twenty-five years.

Steve has an extensive history of exploration and travel. Born in Midwest America (Detroit), he spent the next twenty-five years of his life living in many urban and nonurban places throughout the U.S. mainland—from the Midwest (Illinois, Michigan) to the South (North Carolina, Georgia, Texas), out West (northern California) and to the eastern seaboard (New Jersey, Maryland, Delaware)—and even spent six years in the Caribbean (Puerto Rico, Saint Thomas). Fueling an intense interest to learn about new cultures and to connect with people from all walks of life, Steve's professional career with UBS continued on where he left off, taking extensive business assignments throughout the world (Sweden, Switzerland, Germany, United Kingdom, and Japan).

Starting his career with UBS as a software engineer, and with his unique perspective on the strengths of different cultures as well as the issues of cultural barriers to change, Steve's responsibilities evolved from software development to change program management, to department head of a global logistics team of more than one hundred people, and finally into the lead role for a business advisory service in knowledge management. Throughout this evolution, Steve has worked in many logistics areas supporting UBS's core businesses and has built up an extensive knowledge of banking and an incredible network of experts around the world that he works with daily. It is this hands-on experience in technology development and organizational change management, along with his acumen in cultural growth, that has crystallized into the evolving business strategy of *The Wisdom Network.*

Melissa Giovagnoli is founder and president of the consulting firm Networlding and The Networlding Leadership Resource Center. She is a recognized expert on the development of individual and community leadership networks as a way to grow and accelerate brand loyalty and performance improvement inside and outside organizations. For more than a decade, her company, Networlding, has provided relationship marketing and management programs for organizations like AT&T, CNA, Motorola, and Disney.

Melissa is the author and/or coauthor of ten books, including *Networlding: Building Relationships and Opportunities for Success, The Chicago Entrepreneur's Sourcebook, 75 Cage-Rattling Questions to Change the Way You Work,* and *The Power of Two.* Four of her books have been on top business book lists, including *The Power of Two* and *Networlding,* recognized by Booz Allen as two of the top ten alliance management books.

Melissa has been a guest on both radio and television, including appearances on *The Today Show,* CNN, WGN, CNBC, and FOX. One of her books was featured on *The Oprah Winfrey Show.* She is also a frequent presenter at conferences, specializing in interactive sessions.

With a BA in sociology and a JD from DePaul University College of Law, Melissa founded Service Showcase, Inc., an innovative consulting firm, in 1986. The company's clients now include PricewaterhouseCoopers, AT&T, Dean Foods, and Motorola, as well as dozens of smaller organizations. In 1998 she was chosen one of six extraordinary women of the year by The University of Chicago Women's Graduate Business Alumni Board. Recently she founded The Networlding Leadership Resource Center for Innovation and Collaboration. The Networlding Center offers top leaders both a live and an online community to share wisdom and innovate new products and services. The Center is collaborating with other leadership networks worldwide to create a global innovation network for leaders in organizations of all sizes, from entrepreneurial ventures to Fortune 2000 companies.